Reflecting on the Past

Essays in the History of Youth and Community Work

Edited by

**Ruth Gilchrist, Tracey Hodgson, Tony Jeffs,
Jean Spence, Naomi Stanton and Joyce Walker**

Russell House Publishing

Russell House Publishing
First published in 2011 by:
Russell House Publishing Ltd.
4 St George's House
Uplyme Road
Lyme Regis
Dorset DT7 3LS
Tel: 01297-443948
Fax: 01297-442722
e-mail: help@russellhouse.co.uk
www.russellhouse.co.uk

© Ruth Gilchrist, Tracey Hodgson, Tony Jeffs, Jean Spence, Naomi Stanton and Joyce Walker and the various contributors.

The moral right of Ruth Gilchrist, Tracey Hodgson, Tony Jeffs, Jean Spence, Naomi Stanton and Joyce Walker and the various contributors to be identified as the authors of this work has been asserted by them in accordance with The Copyright Designs and Patents Act 1988.

British Library Cataloguing-in-publication Data:

A catalogue record for this book is available from the British Library.

ISBN: 978-1-903855-73-7

Typeset by TW Typesetting, Plymouth, Devon

Printed by IQ Laserpress, Aldershot

Russell House Publishing

Russell House Publishing aims to publish innovative and valuable materials to help managers, practitioners, trainers, educators and students.
Our full catalogue covers: social policy, working with young people, helping children and families, care of older people, social care, combating social exclusion, revitalising communities and working with offenders.

Full details can be found at www.russellhouse.co.uk and we are pleased to send out information to you by post. Our contact details are on this page.

We are always keen to receive feedback on publications and new ideas for future projects.

Contents

work training programmes or on related courses for social workers, school-teachers and other welfare professionals. Driven from the academy and lecture-hall and excluded from the policy forum, the study of the history of community and youth work has become an oppositional activity. As a branch of learning it will almost certainly be more vigorous and vibrant as a result of that exclusion, but independence and autonomy come at a price. They require individuals to act and co-operate in extending knowledge and understanding. With that in mind, we hope that this small volume will encourage, in some small way, the search for better solutions, more enlightened policies and ways of working that stimulate dialogue and democracy rather than uniformity and conformity.

This book, like earlier volumes, and the conferences to which they are closely linked are self-funding. Consequently many people have contributed their time and labour to make it possible. Therefore the editors would like to put on record their thanks to the contributors. Also to Danny Gilchrist who helped with the design and layout of the cover and Colleen Byrne who worked so hard to make the conference in Minnesota a success.

About the Authors

Simon Bradford Brunel University, School of Sport and Education.

Annette Coburn is a lecturer in Community Education at the University of Strathclyde and is Co-Director of the Scottish Centre for Youth Work Studies.

Dan Conrad retired high school and college teacher, the latter with the Center for Youth Development and Research, University of Minneapolis.

Gabriel Eichsteller is a director of ThemPra Social Pedagogy a social enterprise supporting professionals in relating their practice to social pedagogy.

Ruth Gilchrist is an Education, Training and Development Officer with UK Youth and member of the board of the journal Youth and Policy.

Tracey Hodgson is a member of the Youth and Policy editorial board and a researcher working with Durham University and West End Women and Girls' Centre, Newcastle.

Tony Jeffs an editor of Youth and Policy, part-time teacher Durham University and member of the Institute of Applied Social Research, Bedfordshire University.

Brian McGinley is a lecturer at Strathclyde University and Co-Director of the Scottish Centre for Youth Work Studies.

Sheila Oehrlein is a youth programme co-ordinator for the Minnesota Department of Education and a post-graduate student at the University of Minnesota studying Youth Development Leadership.

Jon Ord teaches Community and Youth Work at the College of St Mark and St John, Plymouth. Previously he was a youth officer with Kingston Youth Service.

CHAPTER 1

The Development of Youth Work With Girls and Young Women in the Nineteenth Century

Tony Jeffs and Jean Spence

The social and charitable activity out of which all youth work emerged can be traced back to the 1770s and 1780s when Britain was moving rapidly from an agricultural to a manufacturing economy, from a rural to an urban society, and when the population was migrating and multiplying at an unprecedented rate. Such changes impacted upon the lives of men, women and children in different ways, disrupting the family-based division of labour and in the process disturbing the social relations of gender and age. The period also witnessed the end of the American and the beginning of the French revolutions, both of which ensnared Britain in protracted and costly conflicts whilst significantly influencing ideas, social relationships and politics at home. Revolutionary ideas about the 'Rights of Man' and 'Liberty, Equality and Fraternity' were contagious, informing political and social turmoil in places far from where they first took root. For those experiencing the changes in the years following 1770, it must indeed have seemed, as Marx and Engels suggested, 'All that is solid melts into air, all that is holy is profaned' (1848: 70).

Inevitably, individuals responded in different and sometimes contradictory ways to the intensity of the upheavals. There were strenuous reactionary efforts on the part of some to hold fast to the old certainties and structures and an enthusiastic engagement on the part of others with the romance of revolutionary activism. Religious revivalism and atheism both challenged the established churches. An outpouring of charitable endeavour amongst individuals and organisations which emerged in response to poverty, distress, social dislocation and conflict was informed by a complex range of motivations. Some activists wished to save souls; others to prevent or encourage political change; perhaps most hoped simply to relieve the suffering of those barely able to survive on the meagre wages paid to factory hands, rural labourers and domestic servants. Meanwhile millenarian ideas, utopianism and socialism combined to various degrees within campaigning movements advocating Jewish enfranchisement, an end to slavery, and as Mary Wollstonecraft (1792) put it, a 'Vindication of the Rights of Women' to set besides Thomas Paine's advocacy of the 'Rights of Man'. Assertive demands for universal male suffrage fuelled the stirrings of a movement arguing for women to be granted political and social equality, and for the first time the rights of children secured a place on the political agenda, notably within the writings of Mary Wollstonecraft and William Godwin.

The Sunday school movement

The organisational beginnings of youth work with girls and young women in the UK emerged from this maelstrom via the Sunday school movement, the founding of which is usually, if somewhat generously attributed to Robert Raikes of Gloucester at around 1780. The early Sunday schools bore little similarity to the placid contemporary version but were more akin to open youth clubs, calculatingly established in acutely deprived neighbourhoods. From the start they embodied some of the key characteristics that subsequently helped define youth work as a discrete activity, namely attendance was voluntary; the educational content was a mix of the formal and informal; the identified clientele were young people; and they offered a combination of education, leisure and welfare provision. The movement was never overly bureaucratic, but Raikes hoped schools would operate according to the precepts catalogued in his original 15 Gloucester Rules, the second of which required 'separate schools for boys and girls' (quoted by Kendall, 1939: 144).

Evidence relating to specific activities for girls can be found in the writings of Sarah Trimmer, a prolific author and pioneer writer of children's fiction, who advocated Sunday schools for girls and young women in the 1780s. Trimmer was a political and religious conservative who believed that social harmony would be fostered by a mingling of the classes and by educating the poor. She held that ignorance, left unaddressed, would amplify existing differences and leave young women from the poorer classes in a state wherein they would 'appear, to those who have had what is called a polite education, little better than a set of savages and barbarians' (Trimmer, 1787: 66). The Sunday school in Brentford which Trimmer established was promoted as an alternative to the temptations of the street and ale-house, as a safe place where a girl might escape from a 'morose father', a 'scolding drunken Mother' and a miserable overcrowded home. As well as offering religious and social education and training, the school provided rudimentary welfare services, including a clothing store, washing facilities and the 'dressing of wounds'. Trimmer described her school as a haven 'where all tears shall be wiped from all eyes, where there are pleasures for evermore', as somewhere to make girls long for the 'return of Sunday' (Trimmer, 1787: 503).

At the beginning of the nineteenth century membership of Sunday schools exceeded 200,000 and expansion continued unabated throughout the century. In an 1835 parliamentary speech, Lord Brougham spoke of 452,000 members (Randall, 1939: 149) and an 1852 survey of Manchester mill workers showed 91.8 per cent to have been members – a figure given credence by a survey undertaken in 1882 which found that 19 per cent of the overall population were currently Sunday school scholars or teachers (Laqueur, 1976: 88–9). Given this level of penetration it is perhaps unsurprising that Sunday schools became the principal model for new organisations directed towards young people and that the influence of Sunday schools can be traced throughout the development of youth work with girls and young women – not least within the religious motivations of the pioneers of such work.

Influence of the Sunday school movement

The establishment of the first recognisable youth clubs is regularly credited to Hannah More who created a dozen or so schools and clubs for young women living in villages across the Mendips during the last two decades of the eighteenth century. These replicated the approach of the Sunday schools in many respects but they operated during weekdays as well as on Sundays and were in a number of characteristics more akin to a club than an instructional school.

Described by a contemporary as the 'most influential woman living in England' (Mellor, 2000: 147) More was a playwright, poet, novelist, prominent abolitionist, religious reformer and close friend of leading cultural and political figures of late eighteenth century Britain including Samuel Johnson, David Garrick, Hester Thrale and William Wilberforce. She was included in a painting by Richard Samuel, completed in 1778, entitled *The Nine Living Muses of Great Britain*, which portrayed the leading women of the age (Eger and Peltz, 2008). Following a spat with a Church of England minister in 1800, who falsely accused her of being unduly well-disposed to Methodism, More was barred from a number of the church halls where her clubs were based and thereafter she continued her work outdoors on village greens and in churchyards (Taylor, 1838). In later years, she became a hard edged evangelical, unsympathetic to radical ideas, reform or liberal writings of any kind. When told by a clergyman that he had burned the volume of Byron's poems containing *Don Juan* she replied that this was insufficient, for she believed the whole *oeuvre* was untouchable (Wilson, 2007). This conservatism was reflected in her work with girls whom she taught to read but not to write, in order that they might study the Bible, but not question their allotted social station.

By the end of the century, with its London headquarters staffed by a team of paid and voluntary workers, a network of full-time secretaries, an extensive property portfolio and world-wide off-shoots, the YWCA was the largest and most professional youth organisation in the world, apart from the YMCA. The scale of the operation and vibrancy of the Association created in approximately three decades without the aid of rapid transport or electronic communication systems, was a triumph of organisational expertise.

YWCA recruitment was focused on members of an emerging class of professional women such as school-mistresses, 'women of business' and their like. Behind the function of servicing the material needs of these young women was the primary desire to 'win their souls for Christ' and to exploit their talents to 'win the souls' of others occupying similar and less exalted social positions. Membership therefore entailed making a commitment to service, for as Robarts explained in an early leaflet 'If we *pray* for others, we must also *work* for them' (reproduced Moor, 1910: 244). This requirement resulted in the YWCA becoming responsible for the operation of a world-wide network of clubs, missions, Sunday schools and social welfare agencies catering for all types of young women, including those not generally viewed as potential members. However, whilst the organisation was inter-denominational, its ethos meant that feminists, those with radical political sympathies and those uncomfortable with an evangelical stance rarely joined. Moreover, given that Robarts spelt out as a pivotal role the freeing of those 'enchained by Judaism, Popery, and heathenism' (quoted Moor 1910: 243–4) those falling into these categories predictably eschewed membership and in some cases found it difficult to collaborate with the YWCA. Yet given its size and presence it could never be ignored and it continued to be represented and to play a leading role in all subsequent developments in work with girls and young women into the twentieth century and beyond.

Rescue organisations

Myriad local and national charities emerged during the nineteenth century anxious to 'rescue' and protect young women from vice, poverty, or loss of faith. Most operated via the medium of home visiting, befriending, outreach, and individualised case-work. Often the focus was highly selective, for example addressing the needs of young women in particular occupations, from specific religious persuasions or residing in a defined locality. For example the Theatrical Mission founded in 1879 by Courtney Todd to work with young women and children employed as actors, dancers and music-hall entertainers (Hope, 1888) met in lodging houses and rented rooms, but also established an Institute in central London. Besides offering residential facilities and a canteen, the Institute was the location for 'clubs' that opened during the day and late at night after the young women finished work.

The Artist's Models Club in Chelsea was a similar venture, but devoid of the Theatrical Mission's religious fervour. It met weekly for social activities and provided a register of approved employers. This Club was founded by Mrs Arnold Glover, later to become the first Honorary Secretary of the National Organisation of Girls' Clubs (NOGC). Some organisations set up residential facilities, such as the 'Working Girls' Homes' whose mission was to save girls from the temptation 'to obtain a few additional shillings from time to time to eke out their scanty little income' for whom 'the temptations are there, real *painfully real*' (*Girls Own Paper* [*GOP*], 1880: 574).[1] The *Girls' Own Paper* itself sponsored 'The Princess Louise Home' and with the aid of subscriptions from readers, established there a laundry 'to enable the girls to help to maintain themselves' (*GOP*, 1885: 442). Other interventions which responded to young women in 'vulnerable' situations, included the *Metropolitan Association for Befriending Young Servants* (MABYS) and the *Girls' Friendly Society* (GFS). These two 'rescue' organisations came to play a prominent role in the development of youth work with girls and young women during the century.

MABYS was founded in 1874 predominately as a consequence of the efforts of Jane Nassau Senior and aimed to find safe domestic employment for girls from workhouses and the poorest homes. Senior, the first paid woman civil servant, pioneering social researcher, a founder of the British Red Cross and proto-feminist reformer, had long campaigned on behalf of workhouse children or the 'children of the state' as she sometimes called them (Oldfield, 2008). MABYS was a practical response to the scandalous way such girls at the age of 12 were sent into the world untrained, uneducated and homeless. Predominately, like poor girls from the provinces without any resources or contacts, they sought domestic work which offered accommodation.

Senior's idea was to release girls from the workhouse into the care of 'ladies' who would befriend them and ensure they found good safe employment. Meanwhile, those arriving at the metropolitan railway termini in search of work would be met by accredited women workers from the *Traveller's Aid Society*, (founded by the YWCA)[2] and then found temporary accommodation, suitable employment and a lady visitor by MABYS. Frances Power Cobbe, who had launched a similar scheme in Bristol recalled the sentiments of this approach as: 'Let us make the girls, first safe; then as happy as we can' (Power Cobbe, 1904: 337). Each lady befriended no more than eight girls. She was expected to 'inspect' their workplace at least monthly to ensure they were being well treated, were safe and properly trained; to help with practical matters such as clothing; and to invite them to her own home for social occasions. When young women moved on, their details were passed onto another lady visitor via district committees.

MABYS lodges were established to provide residential accommodation for young women 'awaiting' or between employment, and as a facility where they could go for the 'remains of the day'. Generally these had lounges, libraries and facilities for bathing and doing their laundry. MABYS clubs were also run by settlements and missions for the young women. By the mid-1890s MABYS had 1,000 ladies befriending 8,000 protégées, 30 district committees and 22 lodges. Whereas prior to its launch a survey had found that all 80 workhouse girls it traced were living 'on the streets', by 1895 MABYS claimed that 70 per cent were still in contact with the organisation and working in safe secure domestic employment by age 20 (Pratt, 1897).

Margaret Elliot, who had previously worked with Mary Carpenter and Frances Power Cobbe in Bristol, and was one of the members of the founding committee of MABYS recalled in her biography:

> . . . with feelings of pride and gratification that up to 1877, when the difficulties of launching the undertaking had been overcome, and influential support obtained, we were all women, No man was on the Council; we had no officer connected with our work but women.

> (Elliot, 1894: 7)

Whilst MABYS operated solely within London, the Girls' Friendly Society (GFS) was to become a national organisation. In 1874 Mary Townsend, the daughter of a vicar and wife of a Warwickshire landowner and MP, met with four others, including Jane Nassau Senior, to establish a body to undertake similar work to that of MABYS in the rest of the country. Senior died three years later, but it is likely her involvement in the new organisation would have been fleeting, for although it adopted a similar working methodology to MABYS it operated according to different principles. First, whereas Senior had pledged that MABYS would operate on a non-denominational basis, the GFS from the start was incorporated within the structure of the Church of England and organised on a Diocesan basis with a branch representing a single or group of parishes. This arrangement enabled it to grow rapidly as it incorporated a number of parish based organisations already working to ensure the purity of girls and young women (Money, 1897; Heath-Stubbs, 1926). By 1885 there were 820 branches in operation. However over time this link with the Church was to severely restrict the reach of the GFS. Second, according to its founder, GFS was motivated by a 'threefold ideal – the witness for purity, the power of friendliness, and the bond of intercession' (quoted Townend, 1923: 36). The first of these meant that one of the Central Rules of the GFS laid down that 'No girl who has not borne a virtuous character to be admitted as a member; such character being lost, the member to forfeit her card'. Consequently the organisation focused only on those girls and young women considered to be 'respectable', insisting that there were already 'many agencies at work in raising

Mrs Townsend: GFS founder

the fallen' (Pratt, 1897: 235). The priority for GFS was always to focus on the preservation of 'purity'.

The GFS comprised members; candidates (girls over eight but below 13 and therefore too young to be members); and Associates, women who agreed to look after members and candidates. Often Associates took their responsibilities most seriously and such was their willingness to ensure that employers treated their servants in an acceptable fashion that in some circles it became known as the Great Fuss Society and adverts were known to appear citing 'No GFS members need apply' (Fabes and Skinner, 2001). As the GFS grew, so the structure was segmented into a format that reflected the various foci of the organisation and the social divisions amongst the membership. By the 1890s it embodied ten departments catering for discrete groups and needs who were:

- Members in professions and business for whom there were sub-divisions for teachers, nurses, music and art students and shop assistants.
- Members in mills, factories and warehouses.
- Candidates from workhouses in the provinces and orphanages.
- Members in service.
- Registry work.

time residing 'outside the demands of work, direct social obligations and the routine activities of personal and domestic maintenance' (Bailey, 1978: 6). The lives of girls and young women were additionally circumscribed by domestic responsibilities and the assumption that they ought to spend their time at home. Discussing the reasons why children attended Sunday schools, one *GOP* article suggested that for some 'perhaps . . . it is less trouble than to nurse the baby or help mother at home' (*GOP*, 1880a: 282). Boys enjoyed more leisure time and for that reason were viewed as simultaneously being a greater threat to social order and at greater risk of corruption by denizens of the streets. Therefore the focus of youth work on the needs of young men partially reflected the extent that they, unlike many young women, escaped the double burden of work beyond and within the home. As mechanisation, trade union agitation and legislation combined to reduce the working hours of the factory hand so the leisure time enjoyed by young men expanded. For young women this was much less so, for fewer hours spent at the factory usually translated into more hours devoted to domestic labour. Where it did not, and when working class girls spent leisure time outside the home, they were deemed to be risking their respectability. Girls clubs and organisations were especially significant for girls in these terms.

Particular issues emerged with regard to the realities of waged employment for young women during the period encompassing the years between 1850 and the outbreak of war in 1914. Prior to that time over a third of young women were employed as domestic servants and roughly an equal number as home workers, in retail trades and in sweated industries located in small workshops. Pethick Lawrence recalled that girls attending the West London Mission Club predominately worked in the clothing trade, 11 to 12 hours a day, six days a week (1938: 78). All their principal occupations were un-unionised and largely escaped existing employment law or the scrutiny of factory inspectors. Contemporary commentators stressed the meager earnings of young women (e.g. Montagu, 1904; *GOP*, 1880). Outside the mill towns young women were not considered to be serious employees but merely to be biding their time until marriage. What was left of their wages after paying rent to a landlord or board to a parent was so sparse according to Stanley that during their leisure time they had nothing to hand but 'rough play with boys and lads', walking around and 'looking in shops' and if a few pence came their way visiting 'the music-hall, the cheap theatres, the gin palaces, the dancing saloons and the wine shop' (Stanley, 1890: 13) activities which were considered to expose them to moral dangers.

Paradoxically it was young women who were far more likely to leave home to seek employment. Flora Thompson notes in her account of life in rural Oxfordshire in the 1870s that whilst boys and young men were kept at home for their superior earning power:

There was no girl over twelve or thirteen living permanently at home. Some were sent out to their first place at eleven. The way they were pushed out into the world at that tender age might have seemed heartless to a casual observer. As soon as a little girl approached school-leaving age, her mother would say, 'about time you was earnin' your own livin', me gal' . . . The parents did not want the boys to leave home.

(1939: 155)

The poorer and less educated left to enter service, the next 'layer' to work in and frequently live above, shops or department stores. J.M. Keynes (1911) found that all the boys who left the Cambridge elementary schools in 1908 and 1909 were resident in the city come October 1910 (see also Freeman, 1914) this was at a time when as many as a third of young women of similar age were living away from their family home (Collier, 1918).

Such patterns of work and 'leisure' prompted youth work with young women to progress along distinctive lines. The consistent boys' club aspiration of a purpose-built unit open seven nights and weekends offering a programme of sporting activities, classes and leisure pursuits plus teams competing in local leagues, co-ordinated by a full-time leader was inappropriate for young women with little if any leisure time. Those working with young women fashioned different models of intervention. Workers visited factories and shops to hold 'Dinner-Hour Meetings' (Kumm, ud.) ladies from the MABYS and the GFS visited young women, especially those in domestic service at their place of employment and invited them to meetings and tea in their own homes; workers opened rest-rooms in or adjacent to places of employment; equipped caravans to visit isolated country homes and villages; provided houses where servants and shop-girls might go on their day off to relax and socialise; organised single-evening clubs in rented rooms, settlements, missions, schools and church halls; worked with small groups that met at the home of the worker; and organised Saturday afternoon and Sunday activities and summer rambles. Few girls' clubs were located in specially adapted or purpose-built units, and probably few saw a need for such centres. The only significant exception to this was the YWCAs catering for 'respectable' young women in business, teaching, nursing and other elite forms of 'womanly' employment who enjoyed above-average leisure-time and were not required to perform household chores in their own parents' home. Such women therefore had both the time to devote to an organisation that expected members to contribute to its corporate life, and an income sufficient to pay the annual membership fee, equal to a police officer's weekly wage.

The relationship between work, leisure, domesticity and public life was entirely different for young men and young women of whatever class. The interest of social commentators was aroused by a broad range of issues associated with male youth culminating in numerous sociological studies associated with the 'boy' problem in the Edwardian period. There was never an equivalent 'girl problem' and Lily Montagu's chapter, 'The Girl in the Background' in Urwick's 1904 collection *Studies of Boy Life in Our Cities*, is aptly titled. The girl, if noticed at all, was generally an afterthought.

Boys had the status robotically accorded the raw material from which the future of the Empire and the economy would be wrought, if well trained they would manufacture ever greater prosperity; if able-bodied they would protect and extend an Empire upon 'which the sun never set'; and if wisely educated they would become mature electors capable of choosing the most perspicacious and prudent legislators. Alternatively, if neglected, they would grow into men lacking in physical and moral character, becoming by default puny physical specimens ill-equipped to execute the arts of industry or war; dangerous and violent and therefore prone to criminal activity; and gullible electors all too easily seduced by counterfeit friends of the poor preaching socialism and insurrection. There did exist an 'underclass' of violent dangerous girls who ran with the city gangs of scuttlers and hooligans who made parts of most urban centres no-go areas for the police and respectable citizenry, but they were negligible in number when set beside their male companions (Davies, 1992; 2008). Their existence nevertheless lent weight to the widespread fears expressed by reformers and social missionaries regarding the dangers posed to young women by music halls, public houses and the temptations of the street. Girls' club workers, such as Lucy Kumm (ud) of the YWCA sponsored Federation of Working Girls' Clubs, who suitably disguised visited these dens of iniquity, did much to publicise these dangers. They missed few opportunities to argue that their clubs offered an effective way 'of counteracting the evils that surround the working classes in large towns' (*The Times*, 27 May 1886, 10).

Whilst young men might be a danger to others on the streets, girls were more likely to be *in* danger. Any leisure time allowed young women was of itself problematic for them. As Stanley argued:

> *How can the working girl find the recreation she must have after ten or eleven hours of monotonous work? The recreation they find loitering around the streets after dark, when work is over, with some chosen companion . . . sometimes rough play with boys and lads, after a time they walk around; looking in shop windows, attracted by the gas lit stalls. Then comes according to their means, a visit to the music hall, the cheap theatres, the gin palaces, the dancing saloons, and the wine shop; then soon follows other temptations, the easy sliding into greater sin, the degradation and downfall of womanly virtue.*
> (1890: 11)

Lucy Kumm and her 'companion' disguised as Factory Girls

Stanley consistently avoided exaggerating the failings of the poor and her autobiographical account of working as a district visitor in the notorious Five Dials area of Soho (1878) stressed the resilience and sacrifices made by women to secure the welfare of their families. For her and many others the pre-eminent challenge arose less from the behaviour of young women living in what another club worker, Emmeline Pethick, called the 'infected areas' of our cities than their relative invisibility (Pethick, 1898). These young women might be loud and boisterous but as Lily Montagu explained, their prime difficulties flowed from the paucity of ambition for self-improvement and the fact that, 'In the economic world the girl's place is inferior to that of the boy' (1904: 237). Even Stanley, when she was questioned by an Inter-Departmental Committee, reported that her initial priority had been to start boy's classes, night schools and Sunday schools before she 'went on to girls' (1904: 488).

Marginalisation meant that girls were addressed less in terms of their character-istics as 'youth' and more with reference to their female condition. Three groups, apart from missionaries seeking converts, paid particular attention to them. These were club and social workers endeavouring to improve and educate young women to become exemplars and 'guides' for their future husbands and children; 'eugenicists fearful of maternal and racial deterioration' (Hendrick, 1994: 5) and wild cat strikes and social disorder. The National Union of Women Workers (NUWW) and the WIC, members of which were to combine to form the NOGC in 1911, both emerged as middle class organisations supporting female trade unionism, and both developed girls' clubs as a means of pursuing their goals. The Organisation Committee of the WIC for instance, in January 1896,:

> . . . decided that to further carry out the resolution that was passed at the conference of club workers, a circular letter should be sent to the leaders of Working Girls' Clubs with a list of questions to be asked of the girls (in an informal manner), regarding the sanitary conditions, hours of labour, fines, deductions &c. It is also asked that any information so gained may be forwarded to the Council, and that in any case of bad sanitation, notice be at once sent to the Sanitary Inspector, or to the WIC.
>
> (*Women's Industrial News* (WIN), 1896: 3)

The Clubs Industrial Association (CIA), founded 3 February 1898 and chaired by Lily Montagu (who carried on this function in the NOGC during its first 12 years) was specifically created by the WIC to promote research concerning industrial conditions for girls, to ensure employer compliance with the Factory Acts and to encourage trade unionism amongst club members.

Fifth, the period witnessed a number of religious revivals and the increasing influence of the social gospel that stirred many to take up club work as a way of evangelising and expressing their faith (Bebbington, 1989; Jeffs, 2005). Bitter experience had suggested that the offer of undiluted religion did not attract many of the girls who were thought to be most in need of intervention. The story of the creation of a 'Girls' Own' Club in the *GOP* notes that a Bible woman 'had started a Bible-class in her room for them, but after one or two attempts, it had dwindled away to nothing'. In creating the new club therefore, the two young middle class volunteers:

> . . . were determined that, since the mere mention of Bible-classes and 'preaching' seemed to frighten the girls away, the class should be at first simply a sort of cross between a night school and a mothers' meeting (without the mothers) hoping to be able to introduce religious teaching by degrees, and to influence the girls for good through many different channels.
>
> (*GOP*, 1880–81: 564)

Although in conventional religious settings the development of clubs increased levels of provision, Booth (1904) found that the insistence of too many clergy that membership must be dependent upon attendance at Bible classes could be a major factor holding back the development of the work.

Finally, the period witnessed the growth of an explicitly feminist movement which highlighted female concerns across the social spectrum from legal disadvantage and lack of rights in marriage, through educational access, to sexual exploitation and child abuse. The central issue in this movement was the vexed question of suffrage, and the women's movement increasingly became identified with the organised struggle for the vote which, according to Emmeline Pethick-Lawrence, inspired a generation of women 'to put into practice in our daily lives some of the highest ideas expressed in philosophies and religions' (quoted in Vicinus, 1985: 285). For many feminists, club work offered a unique avenue to simultaneously influence and serve the younger generation.

Diversity of background and motivation amongst workers and sponsors meant the girls' club movement was always subject to deep abiding schisms. These arose from disagreements relating to religious and political beliefs, but as feminism and the suffrage movement gained momentum, deeply felt differences of position exacerbated the fissures (Bush, 2007; Harrison, 1978). Such divisions caused persistent difficulties regarding the creation of local and national bodies to co-ordinate provision and elevate the profile of girls' clubs. In addition, there remained a bedrock of opposition to club work with girls based upon conservative notions of appropriate female roles. At the British Association Annual Conference in 1904 one speaker, Mrs Grace Steering, pointed out the danger that girls' clubs deprived fathers of the companionship of their daughters and stopped young women from playing with their younger brothers and sisters (*The Times* 23 August 1904). Dolling recalled that the wife of a prominent churchman told him after a lecture:

> *I utterly disapprove of any club that takes girls systematically away from their homes. It makes them for the present unmaidenly, and in the future bad wives and mothers.*

(Dolling, 1896: 38; see also Gomersall, 1997)

The paucity of records means that it is impossible to estimate the number of girls' clubs in existence at the end of the nineteenth century. However, Maude Stanley, who founded the *Girls' Club Union*, estimated there were at least 400 (half the number of boys' clubs) active in London in 1904. Judging by the difficulties in establishing local federations after 1911, and the small number of provincial clubs affiliating to the NOGC before 1914, we can assume that level of provision outside London was lower. Douglas Eyre, Chair of the Federation of Working Lads' Clubs, estimated in 1904 that around five per cent of the youthful members of the industrial classes were 'materially touched or assisted' by clubs (Eyre, 1904: 153). In the same year, a *Twentieth Century League* Survey of 23 Metropolitan Boroughs

In addition to the ubiquitous domestic skill training, club workers were alert to the need for light-heartedness and entertainment in the girls lives. So the programmes also included topics such as millinery, singing, folk dancing, reading circles and games of a sedentary nature. Club leaders organised penny savings banks, clothing and feather clubs. Sometimes there were visiting speakers, single sex and occasionally mixed sex dances, annual outings to the countryside and local visits to places of interest. Speakers were invited to introduce debate and discussion about contemporary issues. Many London clubs after 1896 had access to a 'circulating library' run by the WIN, the organisation of which was prompted by a gift of books from the Kyrle Society for the benefit of the St Mary-le-Pack Girls' Club (WIN, Oct 1896: 3; *The Times*, 22 Dec 1896). A few clubs had their own libraries, and after the passing of the 1889 Technical Instruction and 1902 Education Acts, progressive LEAs provided teachers for club-based 'extension' classes in approved subjects such as reading and writing, drill and domestic science. Many had a weekly or monthly 'newspaper club' when members read and discussed articles and some, such as *West Central*, provided sex education. Pageants were popular and in the summer many clubs organised rambles that incorporated a visit to the home of a lady who treated members to afternoon tea on the lawn or in her drawing room. Programmes varied enormously, shaped by the resources, the member and leader interests and location.

Two examples may offer a flavour of club life outside London. The first relates to a club linked to Manchester University Settlement with 120 plus members:

> *Classes in needlework etc are held for them. In the autumn they received drilling lessons from Miss Ison, in the mission room of St Philip's Parish, which the vicar was good enough to lend for the purpose. During the summer they are taken to the neighbouring swimming baths.*
>
> (Annual Report of Manchester University Settlement, 1901, quoted in Batsleer, 2003: 77)

The second is a small independent club.

> *My sister and I, together with some dozen or so Leeds girls, have started a Mill Girls' Club in rather a low part of the town. The idea is to give the girls who live in lodgings or have little or nothing to keep them at home in the evenings, a bright pleasant place to come to, out of harm's way. We have taken a large room and made it look as tempting as we can, with bright curtains and some pictures, and above all a very fair piano, which to our musical Yorkshire girls is a source of endless pleasure. Every evening we open at 7, two of us going to superintend, and begin with about an hour's work, sewing and cutting out, reading, writing, etc., on alternate nights. Then we have an hour's games – map, dominoes, draughts, quartettes, etc., and*

*sometimes even a regular romp, when there are not too many there – at 9
we close with a hymn, which generally becomes two or three, and a prayer.
We get from 24 to 30 girls every night, and hear that we have some of the
worst in the neighbourhood. So far, however, they have behaved beautifully,
and we have enjoyed the evenings as much as they. Will you pray that the
work may truly have God's blessing, and that we may be able not only to bring
some happiness into the lives of girls who have so few of our pleasures, but
also to do something towards keeping them from the temptations which seem
so terribly to beset them, and to lead them to know and love our Saviour. One
girl, an orphan, who has not been into a place of worship for a year, has
begun to come to S. School, and Morning and Evening Service. She is a very
bad girl, but one cannot help feeling a liking for at once. Our difficulty is that
unless sharply looked after she uses most dreadful language, and if we cannot
get her to stop, we shall not be able to let her stay in the Club, much as we
want to do her some good.*

(Quoted in Percival, 1951: 59–60)

Depending on size and resources clubs provided rudimentary welfare services. A
doctor or nurse might visit to dispense advice and rudimentary care. In Liverpool
and Manchester prior to 1890 some clubs provided bathing facilities. The West
Central club provided massage sessions for girls whose limbs were tired and
cramped after their day's labour. Many distributed free soap and tooth-brushes and
operated clothing stores. Notably those linked to national organisations such as the
YWCA and the GFS helped members find suitable employment and by using their
contacts with affiliated organisations in the colonies provided assistance to any
seeking to emigrate. *Esperance Girls' Club* set up a co-operative dressmaking
business for unemployed members, paying above average wages for a reduced
working week and using the *WIN* to advertise for custom.

The literature frequently conveys the sense of satisfaction leaders gained from
the work. Often it offered a chance to escape the controlling gaze of men.
Something of this emerges in a later account penned by a Bermondsey settlement
worker who 'revelled':

*. . . in a picturesque lack of respectability, and a freedom in being out of doors
without having dressed for the part which is to me so congenial that the other
day, when Mrs Lidgett looked at me in doubtful surprise as I came wandering
round to the Settlement with neither hat nor gloves, not so much as even the
hall mark of a sunshade, I couldn't think what she was going to scold me for
now.*

(Simmons, 1915: 33)

activities, social interaction and collective responses to problems and issues facing girls and women.

References

Bagot, J. (1904) *Evidence to the Inter-Departmental Committee on Physical Deterioration.* London, House of Commons.

Barnett, H. (1918) *Life of Canon Barnett.* (Vol. 1), London, John Murray.

Batsleer, J. (2003) Practices of Friendship, Youth work and feminist activism in Manchester. In Gilchrist, R., Jeffs, T. and Spence, J. (Eds.) *Architects of Change, Studies in the History of Community and Youth Work*, Leicester, Youth Work Press.

Bebbington, D. (1989) *Evangelicalism in Modern Britain, A History from the 1730s to the 1980s.* London, Routledge.

Booth, C. (1904) *Evidence to the Inter-departmental Committee on Physical Deterioration.* London, House of Commons.

Bush, L. (2007) *Women Against the Vote*, Oxford, Oxford University Press.

Carpenter, M. (1860) *Select Committee on Education of Destitute and Neglected Children, Minutes of Evidence.* London, House of Commons.

Collier, D.J. (1918) *The Girl in Industry.* London, Bell.

Crask, M. (1908) Girl Life in a Slum. *Economic Review*, 18: 184–9.

Davies, A. (1992) *Leisure, Gender and Poverty, Working Class Culture in Salford and Manchester 1900–1939.* Buckingham, Open University Press.

Davies, A. (2008) *The Gangs of Manchester.* Preston, Milo Books.

Dolling, R.R. (1896) *Ten Years in a Portsmouth Slum.* London, Masters and Co.

Dyhouse, C. (1981) *Girls Growing Up in Late Victorian and Edwardian England.* London, RKP.

Eager, W.McG. (1953) *Making Men, The History of Boys' Clubs and Related Movements in Great Britain.* London, University of London Press.

Eger, E. and Peltz, L. (2008) *Brilliant Women, 18th Century Bluestockings.* London, National Portrait Gallery.

Elliot, M. (1894) *Workhouse Girls: Notes of an attempt to help them.* London, Nisbet.

Eyre, D. (1904) *Evidence to the Inter-Departmental Committee on Physical Deterioration.* London, House of Commons.

Fabes, R. and Skinner, A. (2001) The Girls' Friendly Society and the Development of Rural Youth Work 1850–1900. In Gilchrist, R., Jeffs, T. and Spence, J. (Eds.) *Essays in the History of Community and Youth Work*, Leicester, Youth Work Press.

Freeman, A. (1914) *Boy Life and Labour, The Manufacture of Inefficiency.* London, P.S. King.

Freeman, F. (1901) *Religious and Social Work Amongst Girls.* London, Skeffington.

Gomersall, M. (1997) *Working-Class Girls in Nineteenth-Century England, Life, Work and Schooling.* Basingstoke, Macmillan.

Hall, G. Stanley (1904) *Adolescence, Its Psychology and its Relations to Physiology, Anthropology, Sociology, Sex, Crime, Religion and Education (two volumes).* New York, D. Appleton.

Hall, G. Stanley (1923) *Life and Confessions of a Psychologist.* New York, Appleton.

Hargreaves, J. (1994) *Sporting Females, Critical Issues in the History and Sociology of Women's Sports.* London, Routledge.

Harrison, B. (1973) For Church, Queen and Family, The Girls' Friendly Society 1874–1920. *Past and Present*, November, 107–38.

Harrison, B. (1978) *Separate Spheres, The Opposition to Women's Suffrage in Britain*. London, Croom Helm.

Heath-Stubbs, M. (1926) *Friendship's Highway, Being the history of the Girls' Friendly Society 1875–1925*. London, GFS.

Hendrick, H. (1994) *Child Welfare, England 1872–1989*. London, Routledge.

Hendrick, H. (2003) *Child Welfare, Historical Dimensions, Contemporary Debate*. Bristol, Policy Press.

Hope, (Lady) F.S. (1888) *Loving Work in the Highways and Byways*. London, Nelson and Sons.

House of Commons (1904) *Report of the Interdepartmental Committee on Physical Deterioration*. London, House of Commons.

Jeffs, T. (2001) Something to Give and Much to Learn, Settlements and Youth Work. In Gilchrist, R. and Jeffs, T. (Eds.) *Settlements, Social Change and Community Action*. London, Jessica Kingsley.

Jeffs, T. (2003) Basil Henriques and the 'House of Friendship'. In Gilchrist, R., Jeffs, T. and Spence, J. (Eds.) *Architects of Change, Studies in the History of Community and Youth Work*. Leicester, Youth Work Press.

Jeffs, T. (2005) *Newcastle YMCA 150 Years*, Leicester. National Youth Agency/Newcastle-upon-Tyne YMCA.

Jeffs, T. (2006) Oft Referenced, Rarely read? Report of the 1904 Interdepartmental Committee on Physical Deterioration. In Gilchrist, R., Jeffs, T. and Spence, J. (Eds.) *Drawing on the Past: Studies in the History of Community and Youth Work*. Leicester, Youth Work Press.

Kendall, G. (1939) *Robert Raikes*. London, Nicholson and Watson.

Keynes, J.M. (1911) *The Problem of Boy Labour in Cambridge*. Cambridge, Bowes and Bowes.

Koven, S. (1993) Borderlands, Women, Voluntary Action and Child Welfare in Britain, 1840 to 1914. In Koven, S. and Michel, S. (Eds.) *Mothers of a New World, Maternalist Politics and the Origins of Welfare States*. London, Routledge.

Kumm, L. (undated, but c 1907) *In Perils in the City*. London, Headley Brothers.

Laqueur, T.L. (1976) *Religion and Respectability, Sunday Schools and the Working Class Culture 1780–1850*. New Haven, Yale University Press.

Marx, K. and Engels, F. (1848) Manifesto of the Communist Party. In *Marx and Engels, Selected Works*, (1970) London, Lawrence and Wishart.

Mellor, A.K. (2000) *Mothers of the Nation: Women's political writing in England, 1780–1830*. Bloomington, Indiana University Press.

Money, A.L. (1897) *History of the Girls' Friendly Society*. London, Gardner, Darton and Co.

Montagu, L. (1904) The Girl in the Background. In Urwick, E.J. (Ed.) *Studies of Boy Life in Our Cities*. London, J. M. Dent.

Montagu, L. (1954) *My Club and I*. London, Neville Spearman.

Moor, L.M. (1910) *Girls of Yesterday and Today*. London, S.W. Partridge and Co.

Oldfield, S. (2008) *Jeanie, an 'Army of One, Mrs Nassau Senior 1828–1877. The First Woman in Whitehall*. Eastbourne, Sussex Academic Press.

Percival, A. (1951) *Youth Will be Led*. London, Collins.

Pethick, E. (1898) Working Girls' Clubs. In Reason, W. (Ed.) *University and Social Settlements*. London, Methuen.

Pethick-Lawrence, E. (1938) *My Part in Changing the World*. London, Gollancz.

Power Cobbe, F. (1904) *Life of Frances Power Cobbe: As told by herself*. London, Swan Sonnenschein.

Pratt, E.A. (1897) *Pioneer Women in Victoria's Reign*. London, Newnes.

Prochaska, F. (1980) *Women and Philanthropy in Nineteenth Century England*. Oxford, Clarendon.

Prochaska, F. (1988) *The Voluntary Impulse: Philanthropy in Modern Britain*. London, Faber and Faber.

Randall, G. (1939) *Robert Raikes, A Critical Study*. London, Nicholson and Watson.

Reason, W. (1898) *University and Social Settlements*. London, Methuen.

Rose, M. (2001) The Secular Faith of Social Settlements. In Gilchrist, R. and Jeffs, T. (Eds.) *Settlements, Social Change and Community Action*. London, Jessica Kingsley.

Ross, D. (1972) *G Stanley Hall: Psychologist as Prophet*. Chicago University Press.

Ross, E. (2003) A "Lost" Generation: Women's Settlements in London Between the Wars. In Gilchrist, R., Jeffs, T. and Spence, J. (Eds.) *Architects of Change: Studies in the History of Community and Youth Work*. Leicester, Youth Work Press.

Rowbotham, S. (1977) *A New World for Women: Stella Brown: Socialist Feminist*. London, Pluto Press.

Simmons, M. (1915) From St George's House. *Bermondsey Settlement Magazine*, 21, 23.

Slaughter, J.W. (1911) *The Adolescent*. London: Swan Sonnenschein.

Spence, (1998) Lily Montagu: A short biography. *Youth and Policy*, 60, 63–73.

Spence, J. (2003) The Girls' Own Paper and Social Welfare (1880–1908). In Gilchrist, R., Jeffs, T. and Spence, J. (Eds.) *Architects of Change, Studies in the History of Community and Youth Work*. Leicester, Youth Work Press.

Stanley, M. (1878) *Work About the Five Dials*. London, Macmillan.

Stanley, M. (1890) *Clubs for Working Girls*. London, Macmillan.

Stanley, M. (1904) *Evidence to the Inter-Departmental Committee on Physical Deterioration*. London, House of Commons, 488–92.

Stanley, M. (1912) Our Clubs: The Soho Girls' Club. *Girls' Club News*, 3: 1–2.

Stedman Jones, G. (1971) *Outcast London*. Oxford, Clarendon Press.

Taylor, T. (1838) *Memoir of Mrs Hannah More*. London, Joseph Rickerby.

Thompson, F. (1939) *Lark Rise to Candleford*. Oxford, Oxford University Press.

Townend, K.M. (1923) *Some Memories of Mrs Townsend*. London, GFS.

Trimmer, S. (1787) *The Economy of Charity* [reprinted Bibliolife 2009 location not given].

Urwick, E.J. (1904) *Studies of Boy Life in our Cities*. London, J.M. Dent & Co.

Vicinus, M. (1985) *Independent Women, Work and Community for Single Women 1850–1920*. Chicago, University of Chicago Press.

Wilson, B. (2007) *Decency and Disorder, The Age of Cant 1789–1837*. London, Faber.

Wollstonecraft, M. (1792) *A Vindication of the Rights of Women*, http://remnanttrust.ipfw.edu. Document 0368.

Primary Sources

Girls Own Paper (*GOP*) Annuals:

1880, 'The Working Girls of London' (Mrs G.S. Reany, of Reading) Vol. 1, 574).

1880a, 'Sunday School Work', (unattributed) Vol. 1, 282.

1880–81, 'The "Girls' Own" Club, (Dora Hope) Vol. 2, 564.

1885, 'The Princess Louise Home' (Anne Beale), Vol. 6, 442.

1885a, 'The Girls of the World: Facts and Figures' (Emma Brewer) Vol. 6, 346.

1885b, 'Three Social Evenings' (Anne Beale) Vol. 6, 86.

1888, 'How Working Girls Live in London' (Nanette Mason) Vol. 9, 422.

1895, 'Women's Work: Its Value and Possibilities' (F.H.) Vol. 16, 51.

1899–1900, 'Social Incidents in the Life of An East End Girl' (unattributed) Vol. 19–20, 196.

The Times:

27 May 1886

22 Dec 1896

27 July 1903

23 August 1904

Women's Industrial News

Vol 1, (3) Dec 1895: 3.

Vol 1 (4) Jan 1896: 3.

Vol 1 (12) Oct 1896: 3.

Minutes of the Clubs Industrial Association 1896–1903 (Held at LSE Library).

Minutes of the NOGC 1911–1923 (Held at Birmingham University).

Notes

1   The *Girls' Own Paper*, was founded in 1880 by the Society for the Promotion of Christian Knowledge. It became the most popular and widely read magazine for young women at the end of the nineteenth century. The magazine promoted organizations such as the YWCA and the GFS, encouraged 'Parish Work', charitable endeavour and education amongst its readership, and in turn provided opportunities for 'helping' even for those women who lived in isolated and rural areas, or in the outposts of the empire. See Spence (2003) for a discussion of its approach to social work.

2   The Traveller's Aid Society was initiated by the YWCA in 1885 to aid female passengers arriving at ports and railway stations. The managing committee included representative of MABYS, GFS and the National Vigilance Association. Station work continued until 1952 managed by the National Vigilance Association.

3   No contemporary records regarding the details of the Bristol Club or others founded in the 1860s and 1870s are readily to hand. However, given that Hilda Keane was Chairman of the National Council of Girls Clubs (NCGC) in 1936, we must assume she agreed with the accuracy of the information included in the time-line. She also knew personally many of the pioneers some of whom would have 'corrected' such a glaring error. Keane also served as Honorary Treasurer of the NOGC in the 1920s and during her association over four decades with the organization, it is said she visited almost every girls' club in the country (Jeffs, 2011). In addition, given that Margaret Simey, an employee of the NOGC, had her office at the Ancoats Girls' Club in the early 1920s, when Keane was the Treasurer,it is unlikely references to this club are inaccurate. Her opinion must be therefore be given credence.

4   In Britain the ideas of Hall were popularised via the far more accessible writings of J.W. Slaughter (1911).

industrialisation and urbanisation prompted some thinkers and educators to focus on those most in need of welfare. This focus, as Lorenz explains, meant that:

> The social professions in Europe overall have their origins in the fundamental transformation processes that confronted societies with the advent of industrialisation and the political revolutions that replaced feudalism with political systems based on democratic procedures.

> (2008: 628)

The appearance of strong nation states, along with philosophical and political considerations about organising social solidarity, over time fused with a desire amongst some governments to meet minimal welfare obligations to nurture lifelong educational processes for human betterment. However as European welfare regimes evolved differently, the function social pedagogy has fulfilled within them varied.

Historical development in theory and practice

Over time certain strands of thought have combined in the ideas and practice of a number of key thinkers and embodied within their *Haltung* (attitude, ethos or mindset) and, albeit briefly, this chapter introduces some of the most influential thinkers and schools of thought linked to the central concepts of social pedagogy.

Jean-Jacques Rousseau, education in harmony with nature

One of the most significant thinkers was Jean-Jacques Rousseau (1712–1778). Born in Geneva, he lived at a time when children were seen as mini-adults; they wore the same clothes as adults and were expected to contribute to the family's survival by working hard. Their 'childhood' bore little similarity to the cherished period of learning, innocence and safety espoused today. Rousseau's educational philosophy sought to radically change such social concepts (1993 [1762]). He based his theories regarding childhood upon a belief that human beings in their natural state were inherently good but society and its institutions corrupted and denaturalised them. Rousseau viewed the relationship between the individual and society as contentious but argued that society could be improved if children's upbringing was in accordance with nature and its laws. In *Émile*, a novel published in 1762, he described the education of the title character and outlined the principles of an approach emphasising wholeness and harmony with nature. His intention was to preserve the child's 'original perfect nature . . . by means of the careful control of his education and environment, based on an analysis of the different physical and psychological stages through which he passed from birth to maturity' (Stewart and

McCann, 1967: 28). Rousseau's concept of children as perfect due to their proximity to nature radically challenged widely held notions that childhood was a state of being to quickly grow out of and replaced it with a view that it was something worth preserving in an unspoilt form. At a time when education was reserved for the most privileged and was devoted to producing adults, Rousseau innovatively 'argued that the momentum for learning was provided by the growth of the person (nature) – and what the educator needed to do was to facilitate opportunities for learning' (Doyle and Smith, 1997). This emphasis on following the course of nature gave education and upbringing a focus on the everyday life of children in the present rather than persistently looking to the future.

Johann Heinrich Pestalozzi, education of head, heart, and hands

While Rousseau did not put his educational philosophy into practice, his ideas inspired many, notably Johann Heinrich Pestalozzi (1746–1827) who set up several residential schools for orphaned children in order to explore how education could lead to a better civilisation. He refined Rousseau's thoughts by developing a holistic method which sought to educate 'head, heart, and hands' in harmonious unity. Pestalozzi (1819) stated that stimulating children intellectually and arousing their curiosity about the world around them would help form their 'head' and thus their cognitive capacity to think. The moral education of the 'heart' aimed to ensure a 'sense of direction . . . of the inner dignity of our nature, and of the pure, higher, godly being, which lies within us. This sense is not developed by the power of our mind in thought, but is developed by the power of our heart in love' (Heafford, 1967: 61). As the third, and complementary element the 'hands', symbolised that learning is also a physical encounter involving the whole body and all senses, 'physical experiences give rise to mental and spiritual ones' (ibid.: 67). Within Pestalozzi's method the three elements 'head, heart, and hands' are inseparable as:

> Nature forms the child as an indivisible whole, as a vital organic unity with many-sided moral, mental, and physical capacities . . . Each of these capacities is developed through and by means of the others.
>
> (Ibid.: 47)

To be educative in a holistic sense Pestalozzi demanded instruction be based on the individual child's understanding and a 'close observation of children and on deep insight into the way a child's mind works and develops' (ibid.: 46). This form of reflective practice is contained within his doctrine of direct observation or *Anschauung*. Through observation the pedagogue aims to understand the inner resources and potential of the child and thereby support them in their unique natural development. Direct observation is crucial because it is not the pedagogue who forms the child; rather the potentiality of each child is implanted by nature much as a seed contains the design of a tree (Pestalozzi cited in Smith, 2005). The pedagogue's role is to take care 'that no untoward influence shall disturb nature's march of developments' (ibid.). It is an approach that has much in common with the ideas formulated by Rousseau and Comenius.

In addition to his contribution in developing individual pedagogy, Pestalozzi was also influential as a consequence of his self-proclaimed ambition to improve social conditions through the medium of education. Herrmann considers Pestalozzi the 'founder of modern social pedagogy with regards to social learning as opposed to the individual pedagogy that Rousseau established' (1992: 1500). Pestalozzi's ideas relating to family and community education were set forth in his novel *Lienhard and Gertrud* (1819). This described how an economically and morally impoverished community might be re-structured in ways that would enable everyone to live in justice. Key to this was a focus on education for humanity, on realising people's intrinsic potential and enabling them to live their lives as their own creation (Thiersch, 1996). Essentially Pestalozzi's novel creates a Utopian vision of an undamaged, ideal social system. At the same time Pestalozzi demonstrated in *Lienhard and Gertrud* that the community can become a 'new, just, but also socially controlling, instance' (Böhnisch et al., 2005: 26). It also describes Pestalozzi's socio-structural and socio-political approach to reform illustrated through his depiction of an impoverished village community and his concept of education to inform and motivate sociability and economic thinking (Niemeyer, 2002). This explains why both person-centred pedagogues during the New Education Movement discussed later and the proponents of community-oriented pedagogy were influenced by Pestalozzi's ideas.

Paul Natorp, all pedagogy should be social

The term 'social pedagogy' was initially employed by Friedrich Diesterweg and Karl Mager in 1844 to highlight the role of pedagogy in fighting social inequalities. However the German educational philosopher Paul Natorp (1854–1924) was amongst the first to develop social pedagogy in order to find answers to the widely debated social questions of the late 1900s when the industrial revolution, secularisation and urbanisation were creating destitution amongst the expanding working class. Influenced by Plato, Kant and Pestalozzi, Natorp published a monograph in 1894 titled *Religion within the Boundaries of Humanity, A Chapter for the Establishment of Social Pedagogy* (1894). According to Natorp (1894a) the central issue was how to overcome the legally established rule of capital over labour which led to destructive consequences with regards the 'morality' of the entire populace. He argued that the social issues usually linked to poverty were not simply about material hardship but the impoverishment of social existence, and that a lack of social cohesion in Germany caused many social problems. What was needed therefore was a decidedly pedagogic answer to the 'social question', one that reconceptualised the relationship between the individual and society. Referring to Pestalozzi's notion of community education Natorp claimed that 'all pedagogy should be social, that is, that in the philosophy of education the interaction of educational processes and society must be taken into consideration' (Natorp, 1899, cited in Hämäläinen, 2003: 73). This *social* pedagogy should aim to encourage a strong sense of community (*Gemeinschaft*), educate both children and adults to ensure positive relations between the individual and society and fight to close the gap between rich and poor. As Niemeyer (2005) explains Natorp argued that at a theoretical level social pedagogy must research how education is related to social conditions and how social life in the community is affected by educational processes. This meant that the social pedagogue must find the ways and means to design these processes in line with the aim of creating opportunities for those who are educationally disadvantaged and of educating or renewing the community in order that it might develop an individual's morality. Thus Natorp sought to integrate the person- and community-centred aspects of education within his concept of social pedagogy.

The New Education Movement, altering the face of pedagogy

While ongoing inequalities meant that the social aspect of education gained more attention, so did person-centred pedagogy. Pestalozzi's pedagogic philosophy in particular was developed by his student Friedrich Fröbel who initiated the kindergarten movement which raised international awareness of an infant's capacities for learning. Towards the end of the nineteenth and beginning of the twentieth century the ideas of Fröbel and Pestalozzi sparked interest across continental Europe, culminating in the New Education Movement. This looked at ways of transferring these pedagogic concepts into various contexts, including formal education, childcare, residential care and youth work. For example the Italian Maria Montessori, the Austrian Rudolf Steiner and the German Kurt Hahn all developed their own coherent educational philosophy and founded schools based on their principles. The Pole Janusz Korczak set up two orphanages according to similar principles where children had many rights and were compre-hensively involved in running the homes. In youth work, Montessori's method was widely practised and Hahn's philosophies in particular influenced outward bound activities. Hahn also founded the *County Badge* scheme in the UK, now known as the *Duke of Edinburgh's Award*. Many others contributed to international developments of child-centred pedagogic concepts.

The New Education Movement helped foster a discourse that served to gradually establish the nurturing pedagogue as a model for working with children and young people in both formal and informal settings. Within this discourse children came to be conceptualised as equal partners, as resourceful, competent and active agents with their own rights. As one of the most vehement advocates for children's rights, Korczak declared that 'children are not the people of tomorrow, but the people of today' (cited in Joseph, 2007: 19) whilst the Italian Loris Malaguzzi, founder of the Reggio Emilia early childhood learning centres, highlighted children's vast resourcefulness by stating that 'a child has a hundred languages' (cited in Edwards et al., 1998: 3). Children's participation was increasingly seen as fundamental to child-centred pedagogy and was therefore strongly emphasised in the methods of Montessori and Korczak and their followers.

Simultaneously the New Education Movement outlined its ambition to use pedagogy for improving societal conditions by stating two fundamental points, 'First, in all education the personality of the child is an essential concern; second, education must make for human betterment, that is for a New Era' (Boyd and Rawson, 1965: viii). Increasingly a rift occurred between those following in Rousseau's footsteps of child-centred pedagogy who emphasised the first point, and an emerging school of thought that promoted a pedagogy focused on the collective and the community which sought to use pedagogic ideas for social betterment. This debate according to Reyer (2002) was fired by ideological and political discrepancies more than by theoretical differences. Central to the controversy were questions of what was more important – an individual's personal freedom or the collective which required the individual's functional subordination to society – and whether pedagogy was there primarily to educate the individual to become independent or inter-dependent.

Herman Nohl, development of social pedagogy as a humanistic science

As this and other debates developed, different schools of thought emerged. Natorp and his colleagues opened the Marburg School which established the foundations for social pedagogy as a science in its own right. In the 1920s, under the influence of the German educationalist Herman Nohl (1879–1960), it emerged as a 'humanistic science' that sought to develop theories of teaching and learning based on the educational reality in which people live and upon which they base their actions. Hence social pedagogues sought to understand the nature of people's reality, acknowledging that they construct this on the basis of their experiences and perceptions of the world around them. By adopting a hermeneutic perspective they acknowledged that experience is always subjective, and that therefore social problems have a strong subjective element that it is important to recognise when seeking appropriate solutions.

As Lorenz (2008) notes Nohl considered social pedagogy as being brought to life through social movements such as the women's movements and especially the youth movement widespread in Germany during the *Weimar Republic* era, and via social policies that constituted the Weimar Republic's social reconstruction programme after World War I. This had established a democratic constitution which asserted fundamental human rights and basic obligations, which could be linked with Nohl's understanding of social pedagogy as a way of establishing new forms of community underpinned by social obligation.

Social Pedagogy in the Weimar Republic and the National Socialist era

During the Weimar Republic era the 'social question' was reduced to an educational one within the social pedagogic debate (Niemeyer, 2005). Under the influence of the humanistic sciences, the focus of social pedagogy became centred on youth welfare. The first *Youth Welfare Act* (Reichsjugendwohlfahrtsgesetz) in 1924 enshrined children's right to education in a wider sense than just school by establishing their right 'to participate as a citizen in the overall processes of forming a society as a community of "learners"' (Lorenz, 2008: 633). Whereas Natorp (1899) had considered social pedagogy not as a discrete part of education but as a dimension of its entire task, the mainstream definition now followed the principles laid out by the German women's rights advocate and politician Getrud Bäumer (1873–1954) who declared social pedagogy to be a part of the professional field, that is 'everything that is education but not school and not family' (Bäumer, 1929: 3). As Niemeyer (2005) comments, it prospered as a theory of youth work, but this came at a price; whilst the profession expanded the discipline did not – it asked less about educational and socialisation processes and instead focused more on becoming part of institutional and legal structures.

This debate about the individual and the community developed a new dimension with the growth of National Socialism in Germany which highlighted the dangers of collective education controlled by a totalitarian state. The Nazi approach of 'educating' all youths to become part of the 'Volksgemeinschaft' (people's community) took place under the auspices of the 'Hitler Youth' which provided leisure activities paired with nationalist indoctrination. Within social pedagogy Lorenz noted there occurred 'widespread blindness towards the political context and the ensuing separation between social pedagogy as a set of methods and as a social policy framework' (2008: 638). While the leftist political position of some social pedagogic thinkers forced them to leave the German Reich, other academics within the discipline adopted a less oppositional role, by either remaining silent or actively working for the Nazi regime.

Klaus Mollenhauer, towards a critical social pedagogy

The years of Nazi rule left their imprint on German social pedagogy. After 1945 it was obliged to re-evaluate the relationship between the individual and the state. The experience of how easily the Nazis had been able to manipulate wide parts of German society had implications for education. The German pedagogue Klaus Mollenhauer (1928–1998) played a key role in developing critical pedagogy in post-war Germany. According to Niemeyer (2005), during its humanistic science tradition, social pedagogy had been blinded by its own ideology towards political totalitarianism. Mollenhauer pointed out that its autonomy had led to a trivialising and de-politicising of issues which meant it had little pedagogic impact on society. He argued that autonomy should mean being independent in one's pedagogic actions from one's own political, religious and ideological assumptions (Mollenhauer, 1959) but that did not mean denying the socio-political influence of pedagogic practice. According to Mollenhauer (1968) pedagogic relationships and education are necessarily political because they take place in a socio-political context. Education towards human betterment aims to create a model of future society from what exists and therefore requires a critically reflective approach. From Mollenhauer's perspective the aim of social pedagogy was to educate children to take responsibility within their community and to be self-responsible, critical and self-enlightened so they might challenge what they were taught. Society had to be dynamic and democratic and for this purpose the pedagogic task was a dialectic mix of socialisation and liberalisation. He stated that pedagogy should:

> not only conservatively . . . preserve [a] stock of cultural self-evident truths – that a child should be granted his or her right to individual development, be treated in a friendly and not an aggressive manner, gradually gain access to rational argument, learn to interact with friends, a specific form of cleanliness, civilised behaviour and a sense of orderliness – but also to hand down and to produce the means for social change or social progress.
>
> (1964: 28)

It was therefore an approach that would prepare the younger generation for an unforeseeable future.

Hans Thiersch, modern social pedagogy in the lifeworld

In post-war Germany social pedagogy gained influence and strength as a profession as a consequence of significant changes in social and family policy that sought to extend human dignity and solidarity. At the same time the concern with the social problems it had traditionally addressed began to permeate other disciplines such as sociology, psychology and criminology which endeavoured to tackle these empirically (Böhnisch et al., 2005). Therefore social pedagogy was academically viewed as a sub-discipline of these and related social sciences until the socio-political development of the 1960s and 1970s when it established itself as an academic discipline discrete from psychology and sociology. This shift was partly driven by demands from students in Germany and elsewhere to study it as a distinct professional discipline (Lorenz, 2008). Within an increasingly resourceful German welfare state social pedagogy quickly expanded as a profession, widening its scope from child- and family-centred work. This shift supported its emancipation as an academic *inter*-discipline that was separate yet related to others but action-based in its self-conception.

In the late 1970s Hans Thiersch significantly advanced the discipline with his writings on *life-world orientation* ('Lebenswelt-Orientierung') and *everyday-life orientation* ('Alltags-Orientierung'). His article *Everyday-life Practice and Social Pedagogy* (Thiersch, 1978) initiated the development of what has become a core principle of modern social pedagogy in Germany. Rooted in critical hermeneutic pedagogy and symbolic interactionism, life-world orientation is concerned with the everyday experiences of human beings and asks how they can experience themselves as subjects in their own biographies in order to create a successful everyday-life (Grunwald and Thiersch, 2009). As people are part of the society which impacts on the world in which they live their everyday-life social pedagogy has to work at a local/personal level as well as at a societal/political one. It has to see its task as 'constructing the social' in that it must aim to shape and influence social conditions in order to achieve social justice (Thiersch, 2000).

As a result social pedagogic practice 'became more critical, revealing a critical attitude towards society and taking the structural factors of society that produce social suffering into consideration' (Hämäläinen, 2003: 70). In Germany this trend has brought social pedagogy more closely together with social work traditions, and more recently the two have converged to the single, albeit diverse, field of *social care*. The social critical function of social pedagogy has led to its having a particular status in Germany, social pedagogic services are mainly provided by the voluntary sector and are, as a consequence, ideologically independent from the state. Therefore, as the *Child and Youth Welfare Services Act* (1991) explains, the state has the obligation to financially support voluntary organisations in providing welfare services. The public sector is only allowed to provide welfare services directly where no voluntary provider can be found. This system gives voluntary organisations significant autonomy to develop creative social pedagogic practice. Traditionally this also led to practice influencing policies. As there is a wide range

Heafford, M. (1967) *Pestalozzi*, Bungay, Suffolk, Chaucer Press.

Hegstrup, S. (2008) *Tendencies and Trends in Social Pedagogy in Denmark at the Turn of the Millennium*, presentation at the FICE/NCB Conference 'Improving Outcomes for Vulnerable Children and Young People', 18/01/2008.

Herrmann, U. (1992) 'Pestalozzi, Johann Heinrich' in R. Bauer (ed.) *Lexikon des Sozial – und Gesundheitswesens*, Munich, Oldenbourg Verlag.

Joseph, S. (2007) *Loving Every Child, Janusz Korczak*, Chapel Hill, Algonquin.

Lorenz, W. (2008) 'Paradigms and Politics. Understanding Methods Paradigms in an Historical Context:The Case of Social Pedagogy' *The British Journal of Social Work*, 38 (4), 625–44.

Mollenhauer, K. (1959) *Die Ursprünge der Sozialpädagogik in der Industriellen Gesellschaft*, Weinheim, Beltz Verlag.

Mollenhauer, K. (1964) *Einführung in die Sozialpädagogik*, Weinheim, Beltz Verlag.

Mollenhauer, K. (1968) 'Erziehungswirklichkeit' in I. Dahmer and W. Klafki (eds.) *Geisteswissenschaftliche Pädagogik am Ausgang ihrer Epoche – Erich Weniger*, Weinheim, Beltz Verlag.

Moss, P. (2006) 'From a childcare to a pedagogical discourse – or putting care in its place' in J.E. Lewis (ed.), *Children, Changing Families and Welfare States*, Cheltenham, Edward Elgar Publishing.

Natorp, P. (1894) *Religion innerhalb der Grenzen der Humanität, Ein Kapitel zur Grundlegung der Sozialpädagogik*, Freiburg/Leipzig, Mohr.

Natorp, P. (1894a) *Pestalozzis Ideen über Arbeiterbildung und soziale Frage*, Heilbronn, Salzer.

Natorp, P. (1899) 'Sozialpädagogik' in W. Rein (ed.) *Encyclopädisches Handbuch der Pädagogik*, Langensalza, Beltz.

Niemeyer, C. (2002) 'Sozialpädagogik, Sozialarbeit, Soziale Arbeit – ''klassische'' Aspekte der Theoriegeschichte' in W. Thole (ed.) *Grundriss soziale Arbeit*, Opladen, VS Verlag.

Niemeyer, C. (2005) *Klassiker der Sozialpädagogik* (2nd ed.) Weinheim, Juventa Verlag.

Pestalozzi, J. H. (1819) *Lienhard und Gertrud*, Stuttgart, J.G. Cotta.

Petrie, P., Boddy, J., Cameron, C., Wigfall, V. and Simon, A. (2006) *Working with Children in Care-European Perspectives*, Maidenhead, Open University Press.

Regional Youth Work Unit North East (2010) *A Study on the Understanding of Social Pedagogy and its Potential Implications for Youth Work Practice and Training*, Tyne and Wear, RYWU North East.

Reyer, J. (2002) *Kleine Geschichte der Sozialpädagogik. Individuum und Gemeinschaft in der Pädagogik der Moderne*, Schondorg, Schneider Verlag.

Rousseau, J. J. (1993, first published in 1762) *Émile: Or On Education*, London, Phoenix.

Smith, M. K. (2005) 'Johann Heinrich Pestalozzi' *The Online Encyclopaedia of Informal Education*. Available online, http//www.infed.org/thinkers/et-pest.htm (accessed, 20/02/09).

Standish, P. (2004) 'Europe, Continental Philosophy and the Philosophy of Education' *Comparative Education*, 40 (4), 485–501.

Stewart, W. A. C. and McCann, W. P. (1967) *The Educational Innovators, Volume 1 1750–1880*, London, Macmillan.

Thiersch, H. (1978) 'Alltagshandeln und Sozialpädagogik' *Neue Praxis, 25* (1995), 215–34.

Thiersch, H. (1996) 'Sozialarbeitswissenschaft, Neue Herausforderung oder Altbekanntes?' in R. Merten, P. Sommerfeld, T. Koditek (eds.), *Sozialarbeitswissenschaft – Kontroversen und Perspektiven*, Neuwied, Luchterhand.

Thiersch, H. (2000) 'Lebensweltorientierung in der Sozialen Arbeit – als radikalisiertes Programm' in H. Thiersch (ed.) *Positionsbestimmungen der Sozialen Arbeit*, Weinheim, Juventa.

CHAPTER 3

Amelia Earhart, Occupation: Social Worker

Dan Conrad

On Thursday, 21 May 1937, at 3.50 p.m., Amelia Earhart took off from Oakland, California in a twin engine Lockheed Electra to do what no one had tried before: fly around the world at its equator. By late June she was in Lae, New Guinea, with only two stops between there and home. On 1 July, she took off for the first of these, tiny Howland Island in mid-Pacific. As the time for her arrival came and passed, it was clear that something was wrong. Twenty hours into the flight the contact ship *Itasca* received its final radio message from Amelia: 'We cannot see you. We are running out of gas.' She was never heard from again. Not a trace of her, her plane, or her navigator Fred Noonan have ever been found.

It was far from the last the world would hear about Amelia Earhart. Scores of books, thousands of articles and numerous songs, television documentaries and Hollywood feature films have kept her story alive. Nearly 75 years after her death, Amelia Earhart is one of the most recognised names in American history.

A tragic death, even one shrouded in mystery, does not make one an icon unless a remarkable life precedes it. Amelia Earhart was the first woman to fly across the Atlantic as a passenger and then, four years later, the first person since Lindbergh to fly it solo. She was the first to pilot a plane over the Pacific from Hawaii to California, a feat that had claimed the lives of ten others in just the previous two years. She accomplished numerous other 'firsts' and at one point or other held every woman's flying record for altitude, distance, speed and duration.

Throngs of admirers, reporters, and newsreel cameramen followed her wherever she went. She wrote three books, authored scores of articles, designed a line of clothing, gave up to 200 lectures a year and counted among her friends the likes of Lady Nancy Astor in England and Eleanor Roosevelt at home.

Almost lost among the millions of words and thousands of photographs that chronicle her life and death is the fact that at the time she became famous, Amelia Earhart was employed as a social worker at Denison Settlement House in Boston, Massachusetts. She referred to herself as 'a social worker who flies' and it is this Amelia Earhart, the social worker, that is the focus of this chapter.

Still, there would be scant interest in her as a social worker if she were not also an aviator of renown and daring in an era when flying was a grand, glorious and dangerous adventure. That is the point at which the story begins.

The 'Golden Age' of aviation

From the distance of the twenty-first century, it is hard to imagine the excitement surrounding aviation in the early years of the twentieth. Airplanes were frail and flimsy machines that took extraordinary skill, and even more courage, to fly. Nonetheless, there were plenty of people willing to try, and a great many paid the price of a premature death. 'It was an heroic era', aviation historian Sir Peter Masefield recalled.

> *The people who did it became legends not only in their sometimes very short lifetimes but also in aviation history. There's never been anything quite like it since.*

> (Quoted in Mackersley, 1999: 179)

There were many more men than women piloting planes, but it was the women who captured the most attention by their bold foray into what was considered a man's world. The distinction of being the first woman to earn a pilot's license belongs to Baroness Elise de Laroche, a French actress, balloonist, and race car driver who earned her license in Paris in 1910. She was followed by Helene Dutrieux of Belgium who, that same year, went from being a music hall performer and trick cyclist to licensed pilot. The next year Harriet Quimby was licensed in the United States. The age of women pilots was underway.

Flying in the early years was considered a sport and an expensive one at that. Of necessity, therefore, many of the early women flyers were wealthy, and often titled, such as Britain's 'Flying Duchess', the Duchess of Bedford, and Lady Mary Heath. It could also be deadly. Death from a plane crash was the fate of all the above women save Helene Dutrieux.

Among all the pioneering women flyers, two from more humble backgrounds stood tallest among them all. One was a fish merchant's daughter from Kingston upon Hull, Amy Johnson. The other was Amelia Earhart, a social worker from Atchison, Kansas. In 1928, Amelia became famous for being the first woman to cross the Atlantic by air. Two years later, Amy Johnson earned even greater acclaim for her epic solo flight from London to Darwin, Australia. In 1932, Amelia Earhart became the first woman to fly solo across the Atlantic, and later that year Amy was in the headlines for a record-breaking solo flight from London to Cape Town. And so it went as achievements mounted and fame swelled for them both. Despite distances, the two became close friends; a friendship, described in detail by Gillies (2003: 2245–7) that included Amy staying with Amelia for an extended time in New York. Amy Johnson's biographer wrote that the time with Amelia was a turning point for Amy and that she returned from America 'with a new confidence and independence'.

Sadly, these two women would also become linked in the mystery and tragedy of their deaths. In 1937, when Amelia disappeared in the Pacific, Amy was devastated and swore she would never fly again. She wrote to her mother:' No more flights, so no need to worry. "Poor Amelia"' (Gillies, 2003: 302). Three years later, with war intensifying and with it the need for pilots, Amy Johnson did fly again, moving planes around Britain with the Air Transport Authority. Less than a year later she too went down, she too was lost, her body too was never found, and the circumstances surrounding her last flight remain, like Amelia's, shrouded in mystery.

Two amazing women, two remarkable lives, two tragic deaths. But it is to the life of Amelia Earhart, the social worker that flew, that we now turn.

Life experience prepares for social work

Normally it is a risky business to attempt to spot the woman in the girl or the man in the boy. But to find the adventuresome Amelia Earhart in the imaginative,

Amelia's experience as a nurse in Toronto led to a career decision: she would become a doctor. That the career was considered inappropriate for women only fuelled her determination. In the fall of 1919, 22-year-old Amelia entered the pre-med programme at Columbia University in New York. She loved life there and, with her penchant for maths and science, excelled in her studies. But a change in the Earhart family situation put her medical career on hold. Her parents had decided on yet another reconciliation and were living in Los Angeles, California, and pleading with her to join them. Amelia said yes and moved to California, planning to continue her pre-med studies there. It didn't happen. She became a pilot instead.

An account of Amelia Earhart the flyer would now dwell on the four years she lived with her parents in California. For this one, however, it is sufficient to say that her interest in flying developed into a passion and finally a reality. She had her first plane ride there, took flying lessons, earned her pilot's license and through a series of jobs from photographer's assistant to truck driver, she earned the money to purchase her own plane. She flew for sheer joy, did stunt flying in air shows to make money, and along the way set a new women's altitude record of 14,000 feet.

Two years later, another change in family circumstances brought her flying to a halt. Her mother finally decided there was no point in trying to preserve her marriage and, in 1924, the Earharts divorced. Amelia, who for years had been more her mother's caretaker than the reverse, took over again. She sold her plane and truck and bought a flashy yellow convertible that would one day be the delight of children at Denison House. For now, mother and daughter embarked on a leisurely cross-country trip to join younger sister Muriel who was teaching school in Boston, Massachusetts.

Amelia then did what many people in that situation do; she drifted. She re-enrolled in the pre-med programme at Columbia, but lack of money forced her to drop out and abandon her dream of becoming a doctor. She instead took a number of social service jobs. At the time they were her means of survival but, in retrospect, they were more like a series of social work internships and step four in her preparation for social work. She taught trigonometry to blind students, worked as a nurse-companion at a mental hospital, and taught English to immigrants through University Extension. Amelia was now 29, with no more an idea of what she wanted to do, or be, than when she was 20.

Social worker who flies

Fortunately, there was in Boston an organisation that someone in her position could turn to: the Women's Educational and Industrial Union (WEIU). The WEIU was founded in 1877 by Dr Harriet Clisby to support, advocate for, and create new opportunities for women. Harriet Clisby was born in London, educated in Australia, and then moved to the United States where she became one of America's first female physicians. Increasingly distressed over the poverty and general lack of opportunity for women, she left her practice to found the WEIU as a means to address those issues.

When Amelia walked through their doors in 1926, the WEIU was providing a wide range of services for women that included advising and placing college-educated women in fields beyond the usual ones of teaching and nursing. It was just what Amelia needed. The interviewer talked with Amelia only briefly before advising her to apply for a position at Denison Settlement House. When Amelia left, the interviewer penned her notes: 'an extremely interesting girl – very unusual. A writer.' Across the form she wrote in a large scrawl: 'holds a sky pilot's license!?' (Butler, 1997: 125).

It would be interesting to know what was going through Amelia's mind as she neared 93 Tyler Street and the red brick row houses that comprised Denison House. In the 1920s there was no such thing as a social work degree and the term 'social worker' was virtually synonymous with that of settlement worker. What settlement directors were looking for were bright, educated, imaginative, idealistic, and determined women. If they also had life experiences that would help them understand and relate comfortably with the poor, so much the better. Amelia was well-prepared. She may have been thinking that social work was just the career she was seeking.

In 1926, women faced formidable obstacles to entering business, law, medicine and other professional fields and the best and brightest were being drawn instead to social work. It was a field where women could use their initiative, apply their energy and skills, and rise to positions of leadership. There were over 200 settlement houses in the United States and all but a handful were founded, and directed, by women. If things worked out right, Amelia would be entering 'one of the most important professions for women in the early twentieth century' (Spain, 2001: 38).

Denison House was founded in 1892, the third settlement established in the United States. Like the first, Jane Addams' Hull House, it was modelled after Toynbee Hall in London. The founders of Denison House were three professors at prestigious Wellesley Women's College. The most famous of these was Emily Balch who, in 1946, was awarded the Nobel Peace Prize for her work in founding the Women's International League for Peace and Freedom.

By the mid 1920s, the original founders had died or moved on and leadership had been assumed by a second generation of strong, capable, well-educated women. One of these was Marion Perkins, the recently appointed Denison House Head Worker who was waiting to interview Amelia Earhart.

'A tall, slender, boyish-looking young woman walked into my office,' Marion Perkins recalled.

> *She wanted a job and a part-time job would do for she was giving courses in English under the University Extension. She had poise and charm. I liked her quiet sense of humor, the frank direct look in her gray eyes. She had no real experience in social work but she wanted to try it and before I knew it I had engaged her for . . . work at Denison House.*
>
> (Perkins, 2003: XXI, XXII)

Amelia was put in charge of the adult classes in citizenship and English. There were over 100 students enrolled in the evening English classes alone and while she did some teaching her main responsibility was to coordinate the classes and make visits to immigrants' homes. She also organised what we might call support groups, such as her Syrian Women's Club for mothers who had children in programmes at Denison. A few months later, when Amelia moved to other areas of responsibility, she was not ready to give up these contacts and penned a note to Marion Perkins saying:

> *I shall try to keep my contact with the women who have come to class: Mrs S. and her drunken husband, Mrs F.'s struggle to get her husband here, Mrs Z.'s to get her papers in the face of odds, all are problems that are hard to relinquish after a year's friendship.*
>
> (Perkins, 2003: XXII)

Syrian families were just one of the immigrant groups served by Denison House. The neighbourhood had once been largely Irish and then primarily Italian. By the time Amelia arrived the Italian population had largely moved out and been replaced by a mixture of Syrian, Greek and Chinese immigrants. Denison House itself was flanked by a Syrian restaurant on one side and a Chinese restaurant on the other.

Denison, like other settlements, operated under the philosophy that it was not a centre for charity but for democracy. It was an integral part of the community where the staff itself lived and where people could feel at home and consider it their own place. Denison provided a broad mixture of services and opportunities for participation. Some services were offered on a continuing basis such as the citizenship and English classes, job training and placement, the medical clinic, and the kindergarten. Others came and went in response to particular circumstances such as being a meeting place for striking workers or a source of pure milk for babies when that was in short supply.

A basic tenet of settlement philosophy was that immigrant families needed more than jobs, medical care and the like. They also needed music, art, literature, and recreation. You could go to Denison House to gain job skills, but you could also go there for a concert, or a class in Shakespeare, or to study Italian art, or learn to play the violin or piano. The latter was something Amelia could help with as she was a promising pianist as a young girl and later learned to play the mandolin and banjo.

It didn't take long before two things became clear. The first was that Amelia loved social work. She loved being at Denison House, loved the people in the neighbourhood and the comradeship of the staff. Several years later, when she was world famous, she looked back on these friendships and wrote: 'The people whom I met through Denison House were as interesting as any I have ever known' (Earhart, 1977: 53). She illustrated her point by describing her visits, and shared meals, with Syrian and Chinese immigrant families. She wrote this comment, 'as interesting as any I have ever known', two weeks after her solo flight to England where she had met the likes of Winston Churchill, the Prince of Wales and George Bernard Shaw.

The second thing that had become clear was that Amelia Earhart was a very good social worker. She approached her work with boundless enthusiasm and, by early 1927, had moved out of the home she shared with her mother and sister and into a second floor room at the Settlement. It was also apparent that she had a special magic with children. Children, especially girls, followed her around like a Pied Piper. With that in mind, Marion Perkins put her in charge of the pre-kindergarten and of activities for girls ages 5 to 14. This turned out to be what she enjoyed most and where she could apply what Marion Perkins called her 'keen insight into child life' (Wels, 2009: 55).

There were over 600 children involved in classes, clubs, and activities ranging from model building and sewing to choral singing and folk dancing. In addition, all kinds of impromptu events, like volleyball games in the street, would take place after dinner. Amelia's own description captures the flow of a day.

> Each afternoon Denison House swarmed with children released from school. They were of most ages up to fourteen, practically all sizes and several nationalities. I had to see, among other things, that the right children found their way into the right classes, and that game leaders and instructors were on the job and prepared. There were always . . . complications [and]. plaints [sic] from those who never could decide what they really wanted to do always had to be heard.
>
> 'Miss Earhart, I know my lines. Can't I play games today instead of rehearsing the play?'
>
> 'Miss Earhart, I'd rather paint than play games. Please can't I change periods just this once?'
>
> After such temperamental problems were solved for the time, there were others which kept me more or less on the run until dinnertime.
>
> (Earhart, 1977: 58)

Social workers, then as now, were required to develop a statement of goals. In Amelia's overview, she wrote that her aim as a settlement worker was to encourage youth to be 'wide open to all the rich opportunities of life [and] to give boys and girls experiences that will keep them young and that will develop a zest for life' (Perkins, 2003: XXIII). Of particular concern to Amelia were the Syrian and Chinese girls who, she noted, were often 'raised by their families under traditions that cut them off from the freedoms that American girls enjoy.' She was determined, she wrote, 'to open them up to the American experience' (Butler, 1997: 129).

To achieve these goals, Amelia initiated an array of activities. Special interest clubs were formed, the children put on plays and musical productions, and they read and wrote poetry. She also introduced them to the sports she had enjoyed as a child including baseball and tennis. The Syrian girls formed a fencing team and the Chinese girls a basketball team. The Chinese girls were enthusiastic players and became so skilled that Amelia took them to New York to take on settlement teams there.

Amelia, like all social workers, performed many tasks outside her job description. The favourite among the children, was when she would drive up in her battered yellow convertible and pile as many as could safely fit on the seats, fenders and running boards for a slow drive around the block. For many it was their first ride in an automobile and they begged her to drive down their street so they could wave to family and friends gathered on the steps and sidewalk. She also used her sporty car to bring children to and from the hospital and regularly drove a Syrian child to the Perkins Institute for the Blind. Somehow she found extra hours in her week to volunteer there as a reader. Amelia's sister Muriel, thinking back on the days when their grandmother used to bring Atchison orphanage children to her home, recalled:

> Amelia often drove her yellow Kissel car with several teenage girls for a drive to our house . . . for picnics in the yard, or storytelling or marshmallow roasts around the living room fireplace.

> (Morrissey, 1963: 133)

Amid it all there were daily treks up dim tenement stairs for home visits to deal with problems or to just stop by for a chat and share a cup of tea and a pastry. Typically she carried some bright calico to curtain drab windows, a ball for a child or spray of ivy for an older person to tend. On the organisational side, Amelia was soon named to the Denison Board of Directors and became its representative to national settlement conferences.

While all this was going on, Amelia continued to pursue her interest in flying. She kept her flying and social work worlds separate to the degree that most Denison participants and even staff were not aware she was a licensed pilot. Even after generating publicity for a Denison House fund raiser by dropping leaflets over Boston from an airplane, most knew her only as the 'Miss Earhart' who ran their club or taught them fencing or coached their basketball team.

In the summer of 1927, Amelia was named a director of the new airport that opened in Boston. One of her tasks was to demonstrate planes for prospective buyers and this gave her access to planes to fly for fun as well. A completely unplanned flight occurred when a famous female pilot came to Boston for an air show. Several thousand people gathered to watch the airway acrobatics of 23-year-old German stunt pilot Thea Rashe. Her breathtaking exhibition ended abruptly when her plane's engine failed and she crashed to the ground. As soon as Amelia saw she was not injured, she ran to the nearest Waco 10 airplane and took to the air to perform the same loops, spins and dives the featured flyer had planned to perform. Her performance was met with lusty cheers and when asked by reporters why she did it she said she did not want the spectators to leave with the impression that females could not be skilled flyers. Shortly after, the *Boston Evening Telegraph* asked her to provide biographical data for their files on New England pilots. Her data sheet included the usual information of age, education and flying experience. The final category provided the title to this chapter: *Occupation? Social worker* (Butler, 1997: 138).

Amelia the social worker becomes a famous flyer

Amelia was achieving what she had set out to do. She was successful in a career she valued, had weekends and holidays for flying and was becoming well known both as a flyer and a social worker. She may have lived a happy and productive life that most of us would never have heard of if it were not for a phone call she received in early April of 1928. She best describes this turning point in her life herself:

> As for me, I was working as usual around Denison House. The neighbourhood was just pulling in for games and classes and I was as busy as could be. I remember when called to the phone I replied I couldn't answer unless the message was more important than entertaining many little Chinese and Syrian children. The word came assuring me it was.
>
> I excused myself and went to listen to a man's voice ask me whether I was interested in doing something aeronautic which might be hazardous. At first I thought the conversation was a joke, and told the gentleman so. At least twice before I had been approached by bootleggers who promised rich reward . . . I demanded references and got them [and] after checking up made an appointment for late the same day.

(Earhart, 2003: 40, 41)

Amelia must have guessed what the call was about. It had been less than a year since Charles Lindbergh had made his historic solo flight across the Atlantic. In the months since, 18 other attempts had been made and, in the attempts, 14 people had lost their lives. Five women, each hoping to capture the next great first in aviation: to be the first woman to cross the Atlantic by air – as a passenger, had failed to do so. The first to try was a 63-year-old Englishwoman, Princess Lowenstein-Wertheimer. She hired one of England's most accomplished pilots to fly her plane but they disappeared somewhere over the Atlantic. The second was a Viennese actress, Lilli Dillenz, who had the good fortune to be forced to abandon the attempt soon after takeoff. The third was a beauty contest winner from Florida named Ruth Elder who, with her crew, crashed into the sea and were picked up by a Dutch freighter. The fourth was another American, Frances Grayson, a niece of President Woodrow Wilson. She disappeared off the eastern coast of the US. The fifth attempt was by England's most glamorous aviator, Elsie MacKay. She and her pilot set off on 13 March 1928, less than a month before Amelia Earhart received her telephone call. Some 7,000 people waited in New York to greet the woman they knew by her stage and screen name, Poppy Wyndham. Months later a fragment of her plane washed up in Donegal Bay. Amelia was about to be asked to be the sixth woman to attempt the Atlantic crossing.

The person behind the call was Amy Phipps Guest, daughter of a multi-millionaire steel magnate and wife of a British nobleman. After Elsie MacKay disappeared, Amy Guest determined she would finance the sixth attempt. 'I am determined,' she said, 'that an American shall be the first woman to fly across to England. Find me someone nice who will do us proud' (Butler, 1997: 151). One of her advisers called a retired Admiral in Boston to ask if he could think of anyone who might fit the bill. 'Why yes,' he replied,

> I know a young social worker who flies. I'm not sure how many hours she's had, but I know that she's deeply interested in aviation – and a thoroughly fine person. Call Denison House and ask for Amelia Earhart.
>
> (Butler, 1997: 153)

The call was made and Amelia was on her way to her appointment. When Amelia walked through the door, the publicist for Amy Guest got right to the point. Amelia described it this way: '"Should you like to fly the Atlantic?" Such was the greeting I got from Hilton H. Riley who had done the telephoning' (Earhart, 2003: 41). Without hesitation she said yes. She may well have had in mind the poem she had written only days before on the topic of courage. In part it reads:

> Courage is the price that life extracts for granting peace.
> The soul that knows it not, knows not release

From little things;
Knows not the loneliness of fear,
Nor mountain heights where bitter joy can hear
The sound of wings.

The expedition was kept under a veil of secrecy and Amelia was not allowed to tell anyone of the plans and not even her mother and sister knew what was afoot. Meanwhile, it was business as usual for Amelia, the settlement worker. She had recently been made head of the summer programme at Denison and was busy making out the schedule of activities as well as carrying on her usual duties with the kindergarten and the activities for girls. Her arrangement was to take a two-week leave of absence as she fully expected to be back by 1 July. In a note to Marion Perkins she wrote: 'And I'll be back for summer school. I have weighed the values and I want to stay in social work' (Ware, 1993: 42). Her other preparations were to make out her will and pen letters to her mother, father and sister to be delivered in case of her death. In the letter to her sister she wrote: 'I have tried to play for a large stake and if I succeed all will be well. If I don't I shall be happy to pop off in the midst of such an adventure' (Ware, 1993: 42).

The secret of the impending flight was so well kept that when the plane, *The Friendship*, rose out of Boston Harbour in June, there were only three witnesses. Bobbing about in a small boat in the pre-dawn darkness were three social workers from Denison House.

For twenty hours and forty minutes, with Amelia kneeling on the floor or perching on gas cans, the pilots pushed on through storms and fog with only an ordinary compass to guide them. At long last they assumed they must be over land and, virtually out of fuel, dropped below the cloud bank and spotted a welcoming harbour. They brought the plane to a smooth landing in a bay that turned out to be Burry Point, Wales. The sixth woman to try the Atlantic crossing had made it.

The people in that factory town had no idea what or who had arrived so when Amelia waved a white towel as a cry for help, a gentleman on shore waved his coat in cordial reply and walked on. But anonymity was short lived and the whole town was out to greet the crew by the time they stepped on shore. The citizens of Burry Point later erected a monument to commemorate the arrival of Amelia Earhart and it stands there to this day.

That Amelia would be the star of this adventure was inevitable. Try as she might she could not divert attention to the pilot and mechanic who, she fruitlessly attested, deserved all the acclaim. She first tried by saying she was no more important to the flight than a sack of potatoes. When that failed she declared: 'I'm just a social worker on a bat.' The people and the press would have none of it. The *London Times* carried the headline: 'A Woman's Triumph.' Crowds surrounded her wherever she went cheering: 'Well played, my girl, well played.' When she went to shop at Selfridges, having brought no clothes to wear but her flight suit, a cluster of Bobbies was needed to protect her from being crushed by the crowd. She had tea with Prime Minister Stanley Baldwin, shared a platform with Winston Churchill, had a lengthy visit with the Prince of Wales, and addressed the House of Commons. Lady Heath, Britain's flying heroine of the day, took Amelia up for a spin in the Avian airplane she had flown on her record setting flight to and from the Cape – and then sold it to Amelia. Through it all Amelia received hundreds of congratulatory telegrams but no doubt the most important came from Denison House: 'You Know How Our Hearts Have Been With You and Are Staying Right With You Until You Get Back To Us Again Denison House' (Putnam Collection).

And she was, she repeatedly avowed, returning to settlement work as soon as the hoopla died down. On her second day in London she told reporters: 'I don't want merely to be known as the first woman to fly the Atlantic' and, reminding people she was a social worker, went on: 'Aviation is a great thing, but it cannot fill one's life completely . . . I am bringing a message of good will and friendship from American to British settlement houses' (Butler, 1997: 207). She delivered that message in person during her visit to Toynbee Hall which, she later wrote, 'is the dean of settlement houses, on which our own Denison House in Boston is patterned' (Earhart, 2003: 118). On visiting Toynbee Hall she was, at last, received as a social worker and could exchange ideas on settlement work – some of which she jotted down on the back of an envelope: 'Tell Miss P. about Toynbee music groups . . . Toynbee care for babies . . . Hard to get funds here too . . .' (Morrissey, 1963: 161).

Of the many important people she met, she spoke most warmly about the woman she called 'the gracious and brilliant' Lady Nancy Astor. Lady Astor was the first woman to take her seat in the House of Commons and, more to the point, a strong supporter of the settlement movement that went beyond mere words to being founder of the Virginia House Settlement. Amelia described their meeting this way:

> *On my visit to her beautiful country place she led me to a corner and said: 'I am not interested in you a bit because you crossed the Atlantic by air. I want to hear about your settlement work.' I was glad to find someone who regarded me as a human being.*
>
> (Earhart, 1977: 85)

Soon she and her newly acquired Avian plane were aboard ship and headed for New York. A tumultuous greeting awaited her there with sirens blaring and fireboats pumping a water salute in the harbour followed by a triumphal parade up Broadway. The next stop was Boston where a quarter of a million people lined the parade route through town. As Amelia neared familiar ground, the street filled with children from Denison House running along her side yelling in their high pitched voices: 'Hi, Miss Earhart!' 'When can we ride in your car Miss Earhart?' 'Hey, Miss Earhart, it's me, Arfreda!' Later that day she arrived at Denison House and talked for hours with parents, children, and staff. When she finally went to her room on the second floor she was home at last. The next day reporters pumped the children and staff with questions: 'What did she say? What did she think of the flight? How did she like the reception in Boston?' 'We don't know,' came the reply. 'She only asked about us' (Butler, 1997: 204).

It soon became obvious that Amelia was not going to be able to return to her life as a social worker at Denison House. No longer could she casually drop by for tea with an immigrant family as just 'Miss Earhart from the settlement.' The deluge of letters, telegrams, and requests for appearances, and the continuing presence of reporters and autograph-seekers kept her tied up and were disruptive to the work of the House. She confided to her sister: 'I'm afraid my value as a social worker is nil while the hullabaloo keeps up' (Stone, 2007: 75). It did keep up. A short while afterward Amelia packed her things and moved out of Denison House.

Amelia made one more attempt to balance settlement work with fame, lecturing, writing and flying. She had taken a job as aviation editor for *Cosmopolitan* magazine and moved to New York City. She contacted Mary Simkhovitch, head of New York's Greenwich Settlement House and asked if she could live there and join the Greenwich House staff. She wanted, Mary Simkhovitch recalled, to continue her association with social work 'as active as her altered way of life would permit' (Butler, 1997: 221). Ms. Simkhovitch enthusiastically welcomed her and Amelia came to live at 27 Barrow Street as a member of the Greenwich House staff. She ate her meals there and contributed in all the ways she could. Her most active involvement was again with children and girls including coaching a junior girls' basketball team that was victorious in their biggest game of the year.

Susan Butler sums up this moment in Amelia's life as follows:

> *It seemed as if her life were in perfect balance: she was earning her living as a writer, flying when she had the opportunity, and contributing to the social work movement by living in a settlement house.*
>
> (Butler, 1997: 224)

But equilibrium, even a happy and productive one, was not Amelia's style. In August, she took off in the small, open-cockpit plane she had purchased from Lady Heath and headed to California. It was a chance to escape the pressures of fame, clear her mind, think about her future and develop her piloting skills. She called it a mere cross-country vagabond. It was also the first cross-continental flight by a woman and the first solo round trip of the continent by a flyer of either sex. It also made Amelia more in demand than ever. Continuing to combine settlement work with flying, public appearances and writing was no longer feasible. Amelia moved out of Greenwich House and into a women's residence in Manhattan – with her full time secretary. Amelia's days as a settlement worker were over.

Flyer who does social work

Amelia Earhart now faced a dilemma. Her desire to fly and her drive to prove what she, and women generally, could achieve in aviation were stronger than ever. At the same time she loved settlement work and the challenge and sense of purpose being a social worker provided. She needed to find a way to unite her personal drive to succeed with her deep sensitivity to the suffering of others since, as she put it, 'what shuts out happiness for others does so for me and mine' (Butler, 1997: 132).

The solution was actually quite simple, at least in retrospect. She switched from being a social worker who also flies to being a flyer who also does social work. What she had been trying to achieve as a settlement worker she could continue to promote as a flyer. At Denison House her goal had been to encourage a zest in life, to inspire her girls to do and be more than they and others thought possible, and to have the courage to pursue their dreams. It was her aim further, like that of the settlement movement itself, to fight against the social and economic barriers that stood in the way of women fulfilling their dreams. None of these aims had to change, only the means to achieve them.

Amelia Earhart became a flyer with a mission. More than any other single factor that is what set her apart from other accomplished flyers, athletes and movie idols of her day. It is also what makes her life relevant for us today. She always placed her own achievements in a larger context. What she had done, she would insist, was merely an example of what women could do. Her aim was not to be admired, but to inspire. This was her social work, an endeavour she carried out in ways that can only be sketchily illustrated in the rest of this chapter.

Flying for women

At 1.30 p.m. on 21 May 1932, a bright red Lockheed Vega descended from the clouds over Londonderry in Northern Ireland. The plane circled the area for fifteen minutes before touching down among the cows in James Gallagher's pasture. The first to reach the plane was Gallagher's farm hand Dan McCallon who described the scene to reporters the next day:

I couldn't tell whether it was man or woman, but I asked 'Have you flown far?' 'From America' she answered all calm like. I was all stunned and didn't know what else to say.

(NYT, 23 May 1932)

Dan McCallon had just met Amelia Earhart.

The Gallagher pasture was hardly Amelia's original destination, but having endured fierce storms, iced wings, a broken altimeter, blue flame shooting from her left wing, gasoline dripping down her neck from a broken valve and uncertainty about how much fuel she had left, the gently sloping meadow was a welcome sight indeed. She had just become the first woman to fly solo across the Atlantic and the first person after Lindbergh to accomplish the feat.

Word spread quickly from Londonderry to London, and Paramount News sent a plane to escort her to the reception awaiting her there. Perhaps she was just tired, or maybe it was the social worker in her, but she declined. She chose instead to accept the Gallagher's offer of a solid Irish meal and a place to spend the night. When the Gallagher's went to bed that night it probably made no difference to them that the friendly, modest woman asleep on a cot in the back of their humble cottage was the most famous woman in the world.

By next morning a crowd had gathered outside the Gallaghers' cottage and Amelia came out to chat and answer questions, paying most attention to those of the children. Finally she made her goodbyes and joined the people waiting impatiently to take her to London. There she was greeted by swarming crowds that grew only larger as she traveled on to Paris, Rome and Brussels. She had received great acclaim in 1928 as well, but this time it was different. First, she had done something herself. Second, she was ready with a message. 'I chose to fly the Atlantic because I wanted to', she told reporters. 'It was, in a measure . . . a proving to me, and to anyone else interested, that a woman could do it' (Earhart, 1977: 210).

To do something 'because I wanted to' was not, for Amelia, a matter of selfishness but of purposefulness. She said:

> To want in one's heart to do a thing, for its own sake; to enjoy doing it; to concentrate all one's energies upon it – that is not only the surest guarantee of its success. It is also being true to oneself.

(Ware, 1993: 57)

It was the same message she had been delivering to women and girls at every opportunity since the day she arrived at Denison House.

The second part of her statement,' proving a woman could do it', was a message that went beyond the obvious that a woman, given the chance, could pilot a plane as well as a man. It pointed to the whole range of things women were capable of doing of which her accomplishment was merely an example. It was an illustration

Women are physically as qualified for aviation as men, but have to work twice as hard to get the same credit . . . The educational system is based on sex not on aptitude. Many girls find themselves shunted off into cooking and sewing simply because they are girls. In fact I know a great many boys who should be making pies – and a great many girls who would be better off in manual training.

(NYT, 9 May 1931)

To another group of women college students she said:

A girl must nowadays believe completely in herself as an individual. If you want to try a certain job, try it. Then if you find something on the morrow that looks better, make a change. And if you find that you are the first woman to feel an urge in that direction – what does it matter? Act on it just the same.

(Ware, 1993: 130)

Despite the hectic nature of her lecture schedule, Amelia made it a point to include unscheduled and unpaid stops in the cities she visited. When she visited Seattle in 1933, Amelia asked if she could meet with members of the Girl Reserves, a YWCA programme for high school girls. She didn't deliver a lecture, but plopped down on the floor, like the settlement worker she was, for an informal discussion. The group leader related:

None of it was stuffy, , just chatting extemporaneously. Of course, she added, we knew quite well what she was doing and that this was not a chance generosity to a group of girls, but rather a carefully thought out plan to pass on some of her own philosophy and by example to demonstrate that women could achieve whatever they set out to do.

(Ware, 1993: 142)

Each girl also left with an autograph for her scrapbook.

Organising with and advocating for women

Amelia belonged to few organisations but what they had in common is that they were all women's organisations. The ones in which she was the most active were the Ninety Nines (the organisation of women aviators of which she was a founder and its first president) and the National Women's Party (NWP). The NWP was founded by radical suffragist Alice Paul as a means to press a new feminist agenda after suffrage was attained. Their primary focus in the 1930s was passage of the Equal Rights Amendment and they prevailed upon Amelia to be the one to formally present it to the President. Amelia figured prominently in their journal, *Equal Rights*, where they regularly heralded her achievements as 'giving wings to the feminist movement.' In a 1935 issue, the NWP hailed Amelia as 'one of the greatest women of today and the greatest exponent of courage and open-mindedness in our organisation' (Ware, 1993: 123–4).

There were two other issues on which Amelia took a strong public stand. She was an outspoken advocate of birth control and worked often with its most prominent proponent, Margaret Sanger. The other public issue was peace. She had been an outspoken pacifist since she was a young woman and encountered the results of war on the soldiers she cared for in Toronto. She was also an advocate of women being drafted in time of war.

To be a pacifist and to also favour women being drafted was not, for Amelia, a contradiction. For one thing, if women were to be treated equally with men, it should be consistent across the board. But she had a deeper reason which she laid out in her article, *Draft Women for War*:

> *If women go to war with their men, the men are just going to hate it . . . The trenches are the last remaining strongholds of men; and I have a feeling men would rather vacate the arena of war altogether than share it with women.*

(Ware, 1993: 261)

In another article she laid it on with a strong dose of irony:

> *We are citizens paying taxes – which are too largely spent on armaments. So why should we not participate in a military system we help support? . . . To kill, to suffer, to be maimed, wasted, paralyzed, impoverished, to lose mental and physical vigor, to shovel under the dead and to die oneself – 'gloriously.' There is no logic in disqualifying women from such privileges.*

(Ware, 1993: 120–1)

It will never be known what she would have done in the case of Hitler and Nazism. Many of the most outspoken pacifists of the day, such as Emily Balch, founder of the Women's International League for Peace and Freedom (and Denison House) reluctantly made this an exception and supported entry into the Second World War.

Counselling women

Amelia derived her income through a combination of endeavors: lecturing, writing, designing the Amelia Earhart line of clothing, endorsing products, advising aviation companies and the like. She held only two relatively traditional positions in her lifetime: settlement worker at Denison House at the beginning and counsellor to women students at Purdue University in Indiana near the end. There were striking similarities in how she defined her role in both places.

In the 1930s, Dr Edward C. Elliott was president of Purdue University and among his aims for the school was to increase the enrollment of women and to encourage their movement into what at the time were considered the male domains of science, mathematics and engineering. President Elliott met Amelia Earhart in 1934, at the Conference on Current Problems in New York City. They were made for each other. Elliott had a knack for making things happen and Amelia was never one to shy away from a new challenge, especially one aimed at forging new opportunities for women. Just over a year after this meeting, Amelia was on the faculty at Purdue as an advisor to their aviation programme and as a career counsellor for women students.

Amelia's assignment at Purdue included a variety of things but it was her work with women students that she enjoyed most and where she had the greatest impact. Amelia approached this task like the settlement worker of old and chose to live in the Women's Residence Hall on campus. She took her meals in the dining room where girls jockeyed for position to be seated near her. Dinner was often followed by an informal gathering in the residence lounge and more than a few times carried over into Amelia's bedroom where pajama-clad young women would perch on the bed, floor and window ledge to continue their conversation.

Amelia's message to them was the same as ever: You Can Do It! You have choices, you *can* study engineering, and you *can* have a career. It may be difficult but if doors are closed to you, bring an axe! Don't give up your career for early marriage. Graduate first, begin a career, and *then* you might marry – but not to someone who will hold you down or put you into the box your mother is in. Enjoy life, be independent, be free, be true to yourself – and so it would go into the wee hours.

Not everyone was pleased. A faculty wives group complained about the bad example Amelia set by wearing slacks in public and male students complained to Amelia about her advice on marriage saying: 'It's hard enough to get them to marry us as it is'. Faculty members in traditionally male departments like physics and engineering were upset by her encouraging women students to enter their fields.

But Amelia's presence and message was welcomed with enthusiasm by the young women at Purdue. On the news that she would be at Purdue in the fall of 1935, the enrollment of new female students increased so dramatically that the newly constructed Women's Residence Hall turned out to be not nearly large enough to house them. And President Elliott got just what he had wanted and was heard to say: 'Our girls have a real champion to be sure' (Morrissey, 1963: 195).

Conclusion

In the spring of 1936, Amelia received a leave of absence from Purdue for the purpose of preparing for a solo flight around the globe. Barely a year later, she disappeared somewhere in the Pacific Ocean.

How she died is a mystery. How she lived is an inspiration. As a settlement worker she strove to instill in her girls a zest for life – and showed them by her own what that meant. She exhorted women and girls to reach for the stars, to not let people define them or discredit their dreams. Be independent, she exhorted, be free, and dare to be what you truly want to be. If they wondered how they could do it, they only had to look at Amelia.

During her lifetime Amelia received thousands of letters about which she said: 'Best of all the letters . . . are those from average people who have found some measure of satisfaction in the experiment of which I happened to be a small part' (Ware, 1993: 199). All of those letters were lost in a fire but are well represented in the words of one young girl who wrote, for a school assignment, what Amelia meant to her on the occasion of Amelia's visit to her hometown of Port Huron, Michigan in 1934.Thirteen year old Francetta Cole wrote:

> In these days of progress, Miss Earhart leads the way for women who wish to lead freer lives. She is an inspiration to young women who, rather than stay at home in the kitchen, would fly in the air as a bird. One hundred years ago our great-grandmothers had to keep their wings clipped like discontented little birds. A few ugly ducklings flew from the barnyard to become beautiful white swans. Amelia Earhart, as one of these, led the way so that others might dare to follow. We, the women of America, feel gratified that she has shown us a way to make life a more interesting adventure.

(Ware, 1993: 131)

One day, amid the whirl of lectures, receptions and record breaking flights, Amelia was asked if she missed social work. 'No,' she replied, 'since I've never left it.'

References

Butler, S. (1997) *East to the Dawn: The Life of Amelia Earhart*, Cambridge, Massachusetts, Da Capo Press.

Earhart, A. (2003) *20 Hrs. 40 Min.: Our Flight in the Friendship*, Washington D.C., National Geographic Adventure Classics [Original, 1928].

Earhart, A. (1977) *The Fun of It: Random Records of My Own Flying and of Women in Aviation*, Chicago, Academy Chicago Publishers [Original, 1932].

Gillies, M. (2003) *Amy Johnson: Queen of the Air*, London, Weidenfeld and Nicolson.

Mackersley, J. (1999) *'Smithy'.The life of Sir Charles Kingsford Smith*, London,Warner.

Morrissey, M. E. (1963) *Courage is the Price: The Biography of Amelia Earhart*, Wichita, Kansas, McCormick-Armstrong Publishing.

Perkins, M. (2003) 'Introduction by Marion Perkins,' in Earhart, A. *20 Hrs. 40 Min.: Our Flight in the Friendship*, Washington, D.C., National Geographic Adventure Classics [Original, 1928].

Spain, D. (2001) *How Women Saved the City*, Minneapolis, Minnesota, University of Minnesota Press.

Stone, T. (2007) *Amelia Earhart*, New York, DK Publishing.

Ware, S. (1993) *Still Missing: Amelia Earhart and the Search for Modern Feminism*, New York, W. W. Norton & Co.

Wels, S. (2009) *Amelia Earhart: The Thrill of It*. London, Philadelphia, Running Press.

Primary Sources

Putnam Collection of Amelia Earhart Papers, Purdue University.

The New York Times, online archive.

CHAPTER 4

From Raikes' Revolution to Rigid Institution, Sunday Schools in Twentieth Century England

Naomi Stanton

When the Sunday school pioneer Robert Raikes saw a need in his community in the late eighteenth century, his response provoked a 200 year movement the remnants of which still exist today. The young people in Raikes' Gloucestershire community were lacking in basic educational skills, and the community did not like

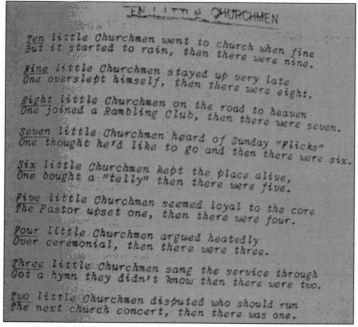

TEN LITTLE CHURCHMEN

Ten little Churchmen went to church when fine
But it started to rain, then there were nine.

Nine little Churchmen stayed up very late
One overslept himself, then there were eight.

Eight little Churchmen on the road to heaven
One joined a Rambling Club, then there were seven.

Seven little Churchmen heard of Sunday "Flicks"
One thought he'd like to go and then there were six.

Six little Churchmen kept the place alive,
One bought a "telly" then there were five.

Five little Churchmen seemed loyal to the core
The Pastor upset one, then there were four.

Four little Churchmen argued heatedly
Over ceremonial, then there were three.

Three little Churchmen sang the service through
Got a hymn they didn't know then there were two.

Two little Churchmen disputed who should run
The next church concert, then there was one.

Birmingham Sunday School Union (BSSU), News, May 1959

these young people 'hanging around' on the streets on a Sunday, their day off from work (Cliff, 1986). Raikes set about responding directly to such concerns by finding teachers willing to spend their Sunday afternoons teaching young people literacy skills. Sunday schools were not attached to churches and conversion was not their primary aim, though the Bible was the key text in their studies (Cliff, 1986). Raikes had identified a need that could be addressed by Christian service. As mainstream education improved and overtook the Sunday schools in Raikes' later life, he intended to replace them with industrial schools to provide young men with the skills they needed for labouring work (Cliff, 1986) but this never happened. Instead, Sunday schools, by now a nation-wide movement, continued as an organisation for the religious education of children and young people. In this form the Sunday schools, now centralised, attached to local churches and accountable to local and national Sunday School Unions, continued to attract attendance from the majority of young people into the early twentieth century (Rosman, 2007).

The twentieth century brought with it some significant changes in engagement with Christianity among children and young people, with the now institutionalised Sunday schools too rigidly structured to respond to their changing needs. Changes that did take place within Sunday schools in the twentieth century reflected the organisational needs of the Sunday School Unions and the churches rather than their young people. Most notable is the move from Sunday school to family church in the mid-century, arguably an attempt to siphon off Sunday school young people into church membership. Possibly this change exacerbated both the decline in attendance and the already present conflict between churches and Sunday School Unions.

This chapter involves an examination of the impact of the shifting religious framework in England in the twentieth century on young people's engagement with organised Christianity, particularly the Sunday school movement's virtual demise in the 1960s. There will also be some comparison with the start of the century when Sunday schools were at their peak in attendance, and the close of the twentieth century. The purpose of this is to explore how young people have engaged with organised Christianity before, during and beyond the pivotal time of religious change in mid-twentieth century England.

Changing context of Christianity in twentieth-century England

Some historians (e.g. Rack, 1969) have assumed that England's Christian frame-work collapsed as a result of industrialisation. However the early 1900s were a time when Christianity was still a massive part of the country's institutional structures, shaping society's moral fabric and legal arrangements. It could be argued that Davie's (1994) concept of 'believing without belonging' attributed by her to many Christians in the latter part of the twentieth century existed at this time in reverse, in that for many it could have been a case of 'belonging without believing'. There was almost certainly a large constituent of those who would fit into a category of 'belonging without questioning'. Bebbington (1989) states that in the nineteenth century, 'Some ministers underwent conversion experiences when already in the ministry' (Bebbington, 1989). Though it should be noted that Bebbington is writing particularly about conversion to Evangelicalism, the fact that many such 'conversion experiences' were documented among clergy demonstrates the strength of the Christian social framework. The fundamental crisis for institutional Christianity would occur when people began to question its rituals, principles, and place in British society.

Despite the apparent security of institutional Christianity in the nineteenth and early twentieth centuries, already there was conflict and insecurity dating from the 1890s when many European countries were separating church from state (Bebbington, 1989; McLeod, 2007a). The sudden collapse of the Christian framework in 1960s England was preceded by similar insecurity. McLeod (2007) points to the impact created by emerging and evolving science, and the looser views and challenges to sexual morality within popular literature at the start of the twentieth century. Rack (1969) suggests that the decline of churchgoing and the keeping of Christian habits was disguised to an extent in the nineteenth century by the growth in population. However Brown (2001) suggests that the true start of the decline of Christendom was not until 1958. Davie (1994) acknowledges the increasing 'religious indifference' of the 1960s. However she also suggests that in the second half of the twentieth century much of the population still held Christian belief but chose not to associate with the institutional church. Davie suggests that, since the mid-twentieth century, many believers choose not to practise an active Christianity but still believe in the Christian God. She describes religious broadcasting such as the ever popular *Songs of Praise* as 'believing without belonging par excellence' (Davie, 1994). Brown's research suggests that the 1960s generation, rejected all but a limited affiliation with church for marriage, baptism and Sunday school and passed even less on to the 1970s generation who retained only the most residual habits and whose children's lives were barely touched by religion (Brown, 2001). This idea that residual belief is not passed through the generations is supported by Cliff (1986) who claims that it only takes two generations to dechristianise a people. Griffiths (2009) recognises the long-held assumption that family (both immediate and including kinship with the wider church community) is the main place where Christianity is passed through the generations. He argues that child evangelism such as that undertaken by the Sunday school movement is a repair strategy when such generationally inherited belief has broken down (Griffiths, 2009).

Twentieth century Sunday school

*. . . the weight of tradition is **heavy**, and we still go on **telling** young people what they **ought** to **know**. But unless they **want** to know what we desire to tell them, our teaching is ineffectual.*

(Hamilton, 1963: 20)

The Sunday school of the twentieth century faced an identity crisis of massive proportions. Many had negotiated the needs and wants of those churches to which they were affiliated as well as the needs of the communities they continued to serve. As society changed the Sunday schools needed to adapt their methods. But they had become so institutionalised in their accountability to the churches and to the rigidly structured Sunday School Unions, that action of any sort could not happen quickly. For example, the minutes of the Brighton Sunday School Union in the early 1900s show that helpers could not be thanked without motions being first proposed and passed at meetings. Similarly, involvement in any kind of external event or new venture required committees to be elected to oversee it (Brighton and District Sunday School Union, Minutes, Oct 1900–December 1911). Writing in the 1940s, Margaret Reeves (cf. Sutcliffe, 2001) acknowledges that the young people of the first half of the twentieth century were subject to many 'conflicting voices' including materialism and political obligation of which their responsibility to church or Sunday school was just one. At a time when the young were beginning to negotiate these priorities for themselves, they needed provision that they had 'planned and led' themselves (Reeves, 1943 cf. Sutcliffe, 2001: 36). However, having sacrificed their autonomy already to church and union authorities the Sunday schools were largely unable to accommodate this. Though the theory of child-centred learning was 'thrown around' in union and church publications for Sunday schools, the Unions did not relinquish enough control to allow the Sunday school teachers to facilitate such education defined by the learner.

Pin-pointing decline

Sunday schools had their peak of attendance in the late nineteenth and early twentieth century (Rosman, 2007; Griffiths, 2009). Rosman (2007: 150) acknowledges that they were still 'substantial organisations' in the early twentieth century stating the example that 'Turn-of-the-century Congregationalists in Westminster Bridge Road, London, organised a total of 15 Sunday schools, nine in the morning and afternoon and six in the evening staffed by 400 teachers and catering for

5,000 students'. However Rosman also notes that Sunday school leaders in the first half of the twentieth century were very much aware of a decline in attendance, but she suggests their reaction was slightly out of proportion when viewed in light of the fact that they were still catering for more children than at the beginning of the previous century. Local records of the East Herts and Birmingham Unions in the early twentieth century reflect a wider concern regarding the education of Sunday school teachers calling for more of them to undertake qualifications specific to the role (EHSU Minutes April 1892–April 1906; BSSU, Monthly Record, January 1905–December 1908). This preoccupation with the training of Sunday school teachers continued into the mid-twentieth century and beyond, and will be considered later. Cliff acknowledges that by the end of the nineteenth century mainstream school education had overtaken Sunday school provision. Robson (2007, 146) acknowledges the claims of Sir Joshua Fitch at the end of the nineteenth century in describing the Sunday school as 'superfluous' if it remained as a supplement to formal education, arguing instead it should become a supplement to family. However it retained its formal structure into the twentieth century. The decline in Sunday school attendance set in despite (and likely because of) a shift to providing specifically Christian education rather than basic skills. Cliff (1986: 322) acknowledges that by the twentieth century Sunday schools were well established as 'an institution for religious conversion'. English nonconformist ministers fought to keep their place as the main provider of religious education over day schools, and succeeded in removing the subject from HMI inspections from 1870 until after 1944 (Robson, 2007: 142). However, Orchard (2007) acknowledges that by the mid-twentieth century the religious education in day schools was of a standard to compete with that offered by Sunday schools, and for many parents was sufficient for their children (Orchard, 2007).

This shift from responding to the self-identifiable needs of its pupils to what could be seen as focusing on the needs of the provider, in terms of filling churches, marks the institutionalisation of the movement and may well be at least partially responsible for its later downfall. Both Cliff (1986) and Rosman (2007) recognise that low numbers of Sunday school graduates progressed to becoming church members. Rosman (2007: 151) states it was not a 'logical corollary' for the young people to progress in this way because Sunday schools were viewed as separate from church services, even after becoming attached to particular churches in the nineteenth century. Cliff (1986: 322) states that the number becoming church members was 'never more than 1 per cent' until the mid-twentieth century when it became slightly higher, presumably due to fewer unchurched young people and a higher percentage of young people from church families attending the schools. However Cliff acknowledges that the success of Sunday schools became measured by the number of conversions or more particularly by members joining the church (which was relatively low) rather than any other enrichment of the lives of those attending.

Other reasons suggested for decline included increasing leisure opportunities on Sunday such as those provided by the television and the motor car (Hamilton, 1963: 14). This focus on blaming external influences may have deflected some churches or Sunday schools away from thinking about internal change. Yeo (1976) looks more widely at society in the late nineteenth and early twentieth century. He claims that society is subject to changing epochs, with certain periods within those epochs having particular influence on culture. He suggests that society was affected by a particular phase of capitalism in the late nineteenth and early twentieth century, that impacted upon people's religious affiliations (Yeo, 1976). Though it may be true that the television and the motor car began to distract the middle classes away from church and Sunday school, Yeo acknowledges this does not account for the lack of the working class population attending church. He recognises the predominately middle-class nature of the church population. Again, blaming external rather than internal problems, he suggests that the 'material culture' of capitalism brought with it a new desire for easy amusement among the labouring classes, often found in drink and gambling. He also suggests there was a new apathy among the population. It can again be highlighted here that it was easier for the religious leaders to blame the people rather than the organisation for decline. However Yeo also claims that the internal decisions of religious bodies reinforced their decline. He talks particularly of the investment in elaborate buildings which many Sunday schools constructed for their classes and various domestic and welfare groups. The maintenance of these buildings marked a shift towards becoming more inward-focused. Subscriptions for attendance could no longer take into account their affordability to all community members but had to be set at a level that covered the costs. Maintaining the building became the priority before funding any new outreach or needs-led work in the community (Yeo, 1976). Orchard (2007) recognises the wealth of social benefits Sunday schools provided in their communities through the groups and activities they ran beyond their Sunday teaching such as temperance groups, adult education and welfare services. He states that the move from a 'communal society to the privatised society' resulted in communities rejecting such help (Orchard, 2007: xvii). The rise of the welfare state also contributed to the redundancy of Sunday schools in their social role. The aspects of social capital originally offered by the Sunday schools were subject to two upheavals: those aspects that became outdated and redundant as society changed, and those increasingly met through a more diverse range of service providers, particularly with the expansion of state funded youth work from 1960 onwards.

Brown (2001) proposes the gender significance of the 1960s religious crisis and is supported by McLeod (2007). It was the first time that as many women as men rejected Christianity. This resulted in a dramatic decline in the passing of religious habits from mother to child down the generations, unlike the temporary crises of previous centuries. This may have led to fewer parents sending their children to Sunday school as both adults in the household disregarded Christianity.

Control issues: institutionalisation versus freedom

Those discussing Sunday school provision in the early twentieth century argued for the need to deformalise their methods and for them to become more holistic and experiential in their practice (see Sutcliffe, 2001). Hamilton Archibald, a Canadian Sunday school pioneer who came to England at this time, stated that 'The Sunday School of the future must be decentralised' (Archibald, 1913–14 cf. Sutcliffe, 2001: 13). Proposals to decrease the authoritarianism of Sunday schooling and encourage children's critical thinking echoed throughout conferences and publications in the early decades (Sutcliffe, 2001). However these ideas were never fully realised and, for most, Sunday school remained a formally structured and controlled occasion to its end. Parker and Hall, commenting in the 1950s, ask:

> Isn't it true to say that generally in Sunday School we talk too much, and that we judge our success and failure by the quietness or noise of the children? We suggest that this over-emphasis on talking is another reason why we lose children. They are bursting with energy, filled with a creative urge and desire to do, their eyes are restless for things to look at – and we seat them in chairs, or on benches, and we want them to be quiet and gain information only by listening to us.
>
> (Parker and Hall, 1950 cf. Sutcliffe, 2001: 40)

It appears that the Sunday schools were aware of the changes needed but never managed to do them.

Alongside these debates for change there was some resistance. As early as 1905, the *Monthly Record*, the Birmingham Union's publication for teachers advocated child-centred education (BSSU, Monthly Record, January 1905). However throughout the same decade it also published a weekly curriculum for Sunday school teaching, providing even an outline for the blackboard, leaving little freedom for teachers to engage in holistic education (BSSU, Monthly Record, February 1909). In the mid-twentieth century, even one of the key proponents of experiential learning in Christian education, H.A. Hamilton criticised the freer Sunday schools (Hamilton, 1963). Writing in 1961 about 'Teenage Religion' after consultation with school leavers about their experiences within formal education, Loukes (1961) appears to acknowledge a need for deinstitutionalisation in religious education. He identifies the need to be 'anti-syllabus' and 'anti-method', to engage more informally with young people (Loukes, 1961: 245). This was something that the Sunday schools had potential to do outside of the formal classroom but they lacked the capacity to rise to the challenge. Griffiths (2009) attributes the success of the early Sunday schools to their use of social currency; of identifying a need within the community, that of responding to the lack of basic education for its young people. Sunday schools of the twentieth century had lost this aspect and he suggests this is, at least in part, responsible for their decline. Without the flexibility to adapt and encompass the social currency of the time and locality in which they served, the teachers were helpless to halt decline.

The centralisation of Sunday schools to churches and Unions occurred in the nineteenth and early twentieth centuries and this attachment may well have contributed to their downfall as it marked a shift in objectives, particularly in their measure of success by numbers becoming church members. Although Sunday schools became, in theory, part of a church, they often retained a 'separate identity' (Sutcliffe, 2001: 28). This may well have caused tensions between the Sunday schools reaching children and young people and the churches still struggling to engage them. Pressure for the Sunday schools to provide church members increased in the twentieth century (Cliff, 1986). Orchard (2007) recognises that there was hostility between churches and Sunday schools with the latter making themselves more accountable to the community than church leadership, and failing to provide church members from their registers. He argues that resentment from churches towards Sunday schools grew after 1945 and included a rising distaste for their traditions and even their name.

The change of name from Sunday School Union to Christian Education in the 1960s may well evidence willingness on the part of the Unions to bridge the gap and break down the Sunday school identity to something more all-encompassing. However the claim by Reeves (1943; cf. Sutcliffe, 2001: 36) when talking about children's part in church fellowship that 'the name Sunday school is now a hindrance and that the Children's Service or Children's Church is more satisfying to the young', is somewhat 'missing the point'. This is because although decline in Sunday school attendance had already begun the Sunday schools certainly struggled less than the churches in engaging young people from non-church families. It would have perhaps been truer to state that the churches considered the name Sunday school to be 'a hindrance' wishing to find something more church-focused as an alternative. Both the Free Churches and the Church of England 'began to turn their attention away from Sunday schools and to a consideration of the responsibility of churches for the Christian education of children' (Sutcliffe, 2001: 39) in the 1950s. This probably increased tensions between the churches and continuing Sunday schools.

Discussion of a new name for the Birmingham Sunday School Union can be traced in their records from August 1962 (BSSU 'News', August 1962). A change of name to the Birmingham Council of Christian Education occurred in February 1966 (Birmingham Council of Christian Education (BCCE), Minutes, February 1966: 87). It could be suggested that if a change of name took four years to accomplish a subsequent change of methods would be far too long a process to be responsive to the immediate concerns of the communities and churches being served. In fact the Birmingham Council minutes of 1967 record a need to amend the constitution before being able to change the teaching materials (BCCE Minutes, 1966: 101).

Yeo (1976) separates religion from the 'religious organisation' – Sunday schools are an example of the latter and it is debatable whether the institutional church is also such. In fact it would be difficult to find within early twentieth century Christianity any form of expression that was not tied up with the rituals and institutionalised traditions of religious organisation. In his reflections on Sunday schools, H.A. Hamilton (1963: 17) argued that 'during the formative years of the child's life he comes to associate religion with the Sunday-school'. It is this concept of Sunday school as representing the whole of religion for children, whilst being a very separate institution from the rest of church-life, that Hamilton held mainly responsible for the problems in recruiting Sunday school graduates to church. He suggested that in outgrowing Sunday school they feel they have also outgrown religion, reinforced by the growing numbers of twentieth century adults having no regular association with the church. Robson (2007: 146) supports this point, stating that 'many men and women linked leaving day school with abandoning the church'. This assumption that Sunday schools were at fault for creating a culture of 'graduating Christianity' may well have served to distract the churches from looking internally for reasons why young people did not opt for church membership in their early adulthood. The fact was that the Sunday schools were successfully engaging large numbers of young people well into the twentieth century – but the churches were failing to attract them into adult membership.

Following the mid-twentieth century decline of Sunday schools, rather than mourn this, many church publications appeared to blame it for the lack of young people in the church. Francis et al highlight several documents published in the 1970s and 1980s that exhibited negative attitudes towards the Sunday school movement of the earlier decades, even going as far as regarding its decline a 'blessing in disguise' (Nixon, 1985; cf. Francis et al, 1991: 36). This suggests that perhaps the purposeful affiliation of the churches to Sunday schools in the earlier twentieth century was evidence of the churches attempting to harness the movement, and to exploit its engagement with young people. It may highlight an element of envy from the institutional church towards the Sunday school movement. The church's apparent blaming of Sunday schools for its own inability to retain young people also demonstrates its refusal to look for reasons within itself. The churches are surely at more of a disadvantage without the Sunday school movement there to introduce young people to a basic Christian education. Parsons highlights that the decline of Sunday schools has contributed to a decreasing familiarity with Christian doctrine exacerbating the decline of Christendom in British society, though the relation of cause and effect could be questioned here (Parsons, 1994).

Churches were not the only institutional pressures on the Sunday schools; they were also subject to the authority of their local and national Sunday School Union. Local Sunday School Unions began to face financial difficulty in the second half of the twentieth century indicating perhaps that Sunday schools were either closing or choosing not to pay subscriptions for the institutional affiliation to a local union. The costly scripture exam appears to have sapped the finances of some local unions (EHSU Minutes, May 1964). Cliff (1986) acknowledges a growth in the numbers of young people taking the scripture exam even during the period of decline in attendance. It may be that those attending were now more often from a church family and were encouraged in this pursuit. The local union in East Hertfordshire closed in 1965 after finding that its paying subscribers were insufficient to keep the union afloat, with the scripture exam by far the biggest drain on finances (EHSSU Minutes, January 1965). It held a consultation with local Sunday schools on the union's future with a large majority of responses finding it irrelevant and of no use to them. It demonstrates the extent of its institutionalism that the union met regularly with few attendees, and the Sunday schools kept paying for an affiliation they did not find useful simply because they had not yet been asked. The closing of unions is not necessarily a symptom of Sunday school decline but one of changing priorities. It is worth further exploration whether local unions began to close because Sunday school teachers themselves felt they were not of use, or because as they merged with their churches, the churches decided they were not needed. There is archival evidence of conflict between churches and the unions. For example when a local vicar complained to the Birmingham press in the 1960s about a school holding opera rehearsals on a Sunday, the local union's General Secretary responded with disagreement saying the rehearsals did not overlap with Sunday school timings anyway and that the Sunday schools should be looking to share such activities with schools (BSSU Annual General Meetings – enclosed letter, March 1967). Criticism of the churches is evident from the same General Secretary of the Birmingham Union in May 1959 in his editor's letter in News, the union's publication for Sunday school teachers.

It is not surprising perhaps that the unions did not survive as Sunday schools became more closely affiliated with churches if the above is representative of union to church communication.

Several things have raised the question "Are we over organised" or is the B.Y.S.S.U. too far removed from the general conditions of our churches to be of any real service ?   First the question arose at the Youth Conference at Barnes Close, where it was realised that we were presenting ideals to young people who would have little opportunity of putting those ideals into practice in their own churches.   In short, were we wrong in presenting ideals or a forward look to these young christians, which may lead to frustration, rather than achievement ?

Secondly, the question of being "over organised" arose when we had to press so hard to fill the Easter Conference, even with such an attractive programme.

Is the blame with churches who refuse to move with the times, rather than with us being too far ahead ?   Whatever the answer, the fact remains that the church must move faster in this period of rapid social change if it is to communicate the Good News to this day and generation.

Another aspect of this problem is when we find so many results of bad organisation and administration in our Schools and Youth Groups.   Slackness in correspondence, incorrect entries for the Scripture Examination;   is all this indicative of the state of our local church organisation ?   I have heard this word 'indicative' quite often in the office when discussing the many evidences of our difficulties in serving the local church dealing with children and young people.

BSSU, News, May 1959

From Sunday school to family church

In his research Cliff (1986) found that the Sunday schools experienced an increase in members in the 1940s and 50s allowing them to enter the second half of the twentieth century with little concern over numbers or decline. However he attributes the growth in membership merely to the increased birth rate of the time and concludes an underlying decline. Cliff acknowledges that the Sunday school 'movement' was institutionalised by the twentieth century and that it struggled to cope with the cultural transitions of the 1960s and surrounding years. He draws on three cultural 'climates' that effect change in religious education over time as identified by Clifford Jones. These are the 'theological' concerning the 'content' of the education, the 'educational' concerning the 'methods' used and the 'general' concerning the response to the education and its subsequent 'success or failure' (Cliff, 1986: 274). Cliff suggests that the Sunday schools of the 1960s were subject to all of these factors moving against them and that to cope with these changes in parallel was 'too difficult' (Cliff, 1986: 275).

The 1960s were a time of a strategic move towards a 'family church' model instead of separate Sunday schools. Cliff (1986) appears largely in favour of this move. However it may be that at a time when people were rejecting the church this sealed the fate of Sunday schools. It could be argued that the church overall began to withdraw into itself during the 1960s in an attempt to protect itself in the face of increasing criticism. Rosman (2007) recognises that in the 1950s many children were sent to Sunday school despite their parents not being regular attenders at church, but within a few years the 'practice had died out entirely' (Rosman 2007: 157). She attributes the decline of Sunday schools to 'the changing ethos of society' acknowledging that the family church model did not help but suggesting that the demise was inevitable (Rosman 2007: 158).

The nation-wide move to a family church model for Sunday schools was initiated by a 60 page booklet published in the 1940s and again in the early 1960s that proposed and advocated the idea. Although many churches publicly supported the idea from its first mention in the 1940s, it was not entirely embraced by the Sunday School Union until its second dawn in the 1960s (Cliff, 1986). Cliff (1986: 244) criticises the *Sunday School Chronicle*'s editor for 'not liking' the idea and thus not publishing articles about it in its early stages. This illustrates the tensions between church and Sunday School Union with Cliff (1986), a Congregational minister turned Anglican priest, allying himself with the institutional church. The Family Church's proponent and author of the booklet mentioned above, H.A. Hamilton (1963) also an ordained minister, called for a greater unity between Sunday school and church. He claimed that 80 per cent of Sunday school attendees at that time came from non-church families. In light of this figure the disruption to the Sunday school model, particularly its move to fit in with church service times seemed somewhat illogical and the loss of the Sunday school majority inevitable. Arguably, the church saw potential to hijack Sunday schools to feed its own failing youth population. However in reading Hamilton's (1963) outline for the 'principle and practice' of family church it is evident that his ideas were perhaps interpreted more simplistically than he intended. His aim was not merely to change the timing of Sunday school to fit with church services but to change the entire concept of church and the methods employed in engaging and retaining young people in the church family.

Hamilton acknowledged the failings of the churches in attracting young members. He suggests that churches should take more ownership of their affiliated schools and more interest in the young people involved. His objective was for unity between church and Sunday school and he recognised that without a 'spirit of mutual care and understanding' the change in organisation would only serve to have a 'disturbing effect' (Hamilton, 1963: 55). The main thrust of his proposals was a mentorship programme for young people facilitated by church members. The idea involved individual adults in the church 'adopting' individual young people from the Sunday schools. This would include sitting with them in church, being available for conversation, and visiting the young person at home with their family when they started Sunday school and occasionally if, for example, they did not attend. He also believed it was important that church and Sunday school should be combined with young people attending the start of the main church service before their Sunday school programme. He was clear that this did not necessarily mean that Sunday school should fit in with church service times but the opposite if more appropriate. However Hamilton's proposals were not fully met in practice. For some churches, family church may have been seen as an opportunity to retreat or withdraw from supporting a separate Sunday school, or even an opportunity to divert young people into their congregations.

Although Hamilton (1963) presented quite an idealistic picture of how Sunday schooling could be there is some conflict within his theory. For example he appeared at times to be torn between the importance of creativity and syllabus calling for more of the former, and yet a better planned generalised latter. He advocated the fashionable idea of child-centred learning for Sunday schools, yet his proposal of a pre-set generalised curriculum somewhat defied this. There was no mention of recreation in his proposals; his main thrust was for a more conversational approach to learning the Bible rather than for children to be lectured. His writing betrayed a derogatory opinion of teachers and seemed obsessed with the need for better training. Griffiths (2009) similarly criticises the lack of vision and commitment of the twentieth century Sunday school teachers, and the need for training. These arguments are substantiated in the archives by the unions' concern with declining quality of teachers, and calls for them to improve their personal and spiritual lives as well as engage in further training. However it is likely the continual harassment Sunday school teachers faced from their institutional authorities only served to destroy any vision and enthusiasm they held when first taking on the role. The Sunday school teachers employed by Raikes in the 1780s were paid for their work. Twentieth century volunteers may not have felt as valued, confident and competent as Raikes' paid teachers. The social capital passed from Sunday school teachers to pupils had lessened by the mid-twentieth century in that the power division between professional teacher and uneducated learner had eroded. Sunday school members were better educated and increasingly from the middle classes as opposed to the working class scholars of Raikes' time. New volunteer teachers were often recruited from the Sunday school graduates who had not abandoned religion completely.

The records of the national and local Sunday School Unions are frequently punctuated with criticism of the teachers during the twentieth century. For example, as early as 1905, the Birmingham Union's publication for Sunday school teachers, The *Monthly Record*, contains a transcript of the Reverend James Wylie's 'New Year Address to Sunday School Teachers', stating that,

If it is true that the greatest discovery of the nineteenth century was the discovery of the child, it is equally true that one of the chief problems of the twentieth is the evolution of the teacher.

(BSSU, *Monthly Record*, January 1905)

This highlights the conflict between the emergence of child centred learning and the lack of trust in the teachers. The image below comes from the Birmingham Union's publication for teachers in November 1958, now called *News* and emphasises the ongoing message of the incompetence of teachers.

This growing obsession with quality and training came from institutional bodies such as the unions and churches, creating tension with teachers. Hubery (1960 cf. Sutcliffe 2001: 47) suggests that Sunday school teachers were 'aware that the problems of Sunday school cannot be solved entirely by themselves, and rightly resent being regarded as scapegoats for the existence of these problems'.

In his appendices Hamilton (1963) included reports from three churches that had adopted the family church model and deemed it successful. In the first of these there was no mention of increasing numbers of Sunday school attendees or of members joining the church; in fact it stated that those who were not attending Sunday school intending to learn were lost. However the minister deemed the

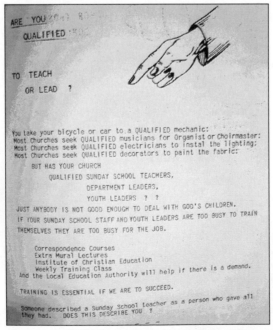

BSSU, News, November 1958

approach a success in bringing the church members and Sunday school children together. The second example from a Superintendent focused less on the contribution of church members (and it is unclear whether the mentorship scheme was adopted) and more on the changing methods within the Sunday school classroom. Through a more child-centred approach they found increases in attendance at all age groups of their school, but this is attributed to increased training for the teachers rather than church unity. There was again no evidence as to whether more pupils went on to become church members. The third example was strongest, coming from a minister whose passion and commitment to the approach was evident. Within seven years Sunday school attendance grew from 180 to 600, though he attributed this at least partially to the post-war birth rates. It is this church that seemed to have most wholly applied Hamilton's ideology. The minister described family church as a 'vision to be interpreted' rather than a 'system to be imposed' (Hamilton, 1963: 62). Though acknowledging some difficulties in the integration process he demonstrated the changing concept of his church in that the word family 'is becoming redundant' as the model became accepted as simply what church is (Hamilton, 1963: 64). However although family church was most successful where it was most fully implemented and changes within the church were made to accommodate children and young people, it is questionable how widely the concept was applied to this extent. Hamilton himself concluded that the mentorship scheme 'proved to be the most difficult to bring to life' (Hamilton, 1963: 63). In the merging of Sunday school and church, Sunday school was bound to take a lower priority. In most cases the church did not adapt as suggested, Sunday school adapted to church, e.g., moving classes from the afternoons to the mornings to fit with established service times. Moving the time may well have made it more expendable to parents if perhaps the childcare element of sending the children out for a couple of hours was less convenient in the morning than the afternoon.

If an element of disharmony and envy did exist between churches and Sunday schools as suggested earlier, then the move to the family church model provided an ideal opportunity for the church to seize power or even to sabotage or bury their affiliated Sunday schools. Cliff (1986) emphasises that Hamilton's observation that 80 per cent of Sunday school members were from non-church families had reversed by the time he died in 1977 to being 80 per cent from church families. This highlights the failure of the strategy to retain the non-church young people. Cliff attributes this to the failure of the church members to become the mentors that Hamilton proposed.

Rosman's (2007) suggestion that the decline of Sunday schools was inevitable even without the move to family church is questionable. Yeo (1976) among others, argues that religious organisations were not just a victim of circumstances, but have agency in defining their future. Given the high proportion of young people from non-church families accessing Sunday schools before the move to family church, it can logically be argued that they might have continued many more years, even decades, without the disruption. If, as suggested earlier, people were primarily rejecting the church rather than Christianity in general in the twentieth century, Sunday schools might have survived had they not succumbed to the pressure to merge with the struggling churches. The adoption of the family church model marks the mid-twentieth century change from Sunday schools as serving a majority of non-church young people to becoming little more than a childcare facility for the adults attending church.

'Tug of War': the role of sport in Sunday schooling

By the beginning of the twentieth century Sunday schools were mainly run by evangelicals (Cliff, 1986). In tracing the history of evangelicalism, Bebbington (1989) demonstrates that in the late nineteenth and early twentieth century there was a rejection of sport, recreation and popular culture within evangelical circles as a distraction from the real cause of their work. Around the same time there was a shift away from social action within evangelicalism and a move to focus solely on preaching the gospel. It was believed that social reform would come after conversion (Bebbington, 1989). Bebbington (1989: 210) recognises the view of this shift in evangelicalism as 'the great reversal' as the evangelical churches became more inward focused. This rejection of recreation inevitably reached the Sunday schools and the new inward looking ministry was a likely precipitant in their decline. Yeo (1976) also pinpoints a move from focusing on the recreational to the devotional within religious organisations in the late nineteenth and early twentieth century. McLeod (2007a) claims that although the notion of Sunday school sports was controversial at the end of the nineteenth century, Sunday school teams in various sports were prevalent in the first three decades of the twentieth century. However he states that they remained separate from Sunday school teaching, often the only link being that the young people had to be members of the Sunday school to join the team. McLeod (2007a) acknowledges that in many cases the teams were without leadership from affiliated teachers or clergy. There is little mention of sport and recreation in the archival records of minute books and documents concerning the direction and administration of Sunday schools. In the Birmingham records, the few mentions there are of sport during the early 1900s and the 1950s and 60s usually refer to the activities of the uniformed brigades, with a publication from February 1912 stating that membership of the Boys' Life Brigade is dependent on attendance at Sunday school (BSSU, *Monthly Record*, February 1912). It appears thus that the main function of sports may have been as a strategy to keep young people in the Sunday schools at an age when many were leaving, as in many cases only those who attended Sunday school that week could play in the subsequent game (McLeod, 2007a). McLeod acknowledges the conflict running throughout the era of Sunday school sport between reaching and retaining young people, particularly the 'Seniors', through means that interested them and the criticism of sport as distracting from what the evangelicals of the time considered to be the pure message of Christianity. The tensions between church authorities and ground-level sports teams led to teams not attached to church-related organisations not being allowed to join leagues, and other restrictions on players related to their attendance (McLeod, 2007a). These constraints, as well as the class divide between church authorities and the working-class sports teams, may well have contributed to the responsibility for youth sports teams being won by independent 'sporting workers' further into the twentieth century (McLeod, 2007a). McLeod also acknowledges that the 'strict sabbatarianism' of many of the Sunday school churches created further tension as Sunday became increasingly a day for recreation. However the legacy of Sunday school sport lives on in teams such as Everton, Aston Villa and Fulham Football Clubs which began as Sunday school teams (BBC, 2008).

Young people and Christianity at the turn of the millennium

The mid-twentieth century decline of the Sunday schools left only seven in every hundred young people attending by 1989 (Rosman, 2007) the majority of whom attended church with Christian parents. Following this, the 1990s saw another 500,000 children and young people leave the Church (Brierley, 2006). The 2005 church census reveals that many churches have no young people at all in their congregations; around half have no 11–14s attending and well over half have no 15–19s (Brierley, 2006). However, significantly, membership of church is no longer the primary measure of success of Christian youth activities. It has been widely recognised that the institutional church is irrelevant to young people by those creating youth activities outside of traditional church boundaries (Clayton and Stanton, 2008). The new movement of youth churches has been successful in recruiting large numbers of young people. For example, the Leeds churches responded to the decline in youth attending their congregations with the creation of a youth church movement outside of the traditional church boundaries. The 'Leeds Youth Cell Network' grew from 10 to 400 regular members between 1999 and 2005 with 36 groups meeting in different locations (Leeds Youth Cell Network, 2008). 'Soul Survivor', probably the largest and most famous of the UK's Christian youth movements, has aged with its congregation as those growing up as young people in the church do not leave for the 'adult' churches. Meeting at a large warehouse in Watford, it has services for adults and families, for students and those in their 20s, as well as their original youth services. It started in 1993 as ten people meeting in a living room and now has around 800 members (Pilavachi, 2009). Their annual summer festival attracted around 21,000 young people from around the UK and abroad in 2009 (Soul Survivor, 2009). Other churches with thriving youth groups are finding themselves creating 18–30s groups as young people outgrow the younger activities; it appears that those growing up in such groups often resist entering 'adult' church.

A publication by the Church of England (1996) acknowledges that the gap between church culture and youth culture increased significantly in the 1990s despite the growing number of youth workers employed by churches. It is significant that in the mid-to-late 1990s there arose a substantial festival movement created to provide opportunities for young people to develop their own styles of worship, evangelism and expressions of faith. In looking at the accessibility of church for young people, the publication cites Bishop Denis Tully who compares young people's feelings of discomfort, insecurity and embarrassment about entering the church's 'open door' to that of some adults approaching public toilets (Church of England, 1996). It is significant that at the beginning of the twentieth century 75 per cent of children and young people accessed Sunday schools with church still at the centre of many communities yet by the end of the century it had become comparable to a public toilet. The gap between church culture and youth culture continues into the twenty-first century acknowledged by research undertaken by the Church of England in 2005 (Savage et al., 2006). The church has responded to decline by what could be seen as the professionalisation of its youth work (Clayton and Stanton, 2008), with the Church of England now employing more full-time youth workers than the state (Brierley, 2003). The danger is that as it becomes more professionalised it becomes institutionalised, as in the twentieth century, inciting further decline. Clayton and Stanton (2008) explore the professionalisation of Christian youth work, acknowledging the growth in numbers of paid workers and the rise of training programmes combining theology with a professional youth work qualification. However they view this professionalising of the sector in light of its move away from the faith-based philanthropic roots of youth work in this country, and question for example whether having professionals both undermines and demotivates volunteers. The professionalisation of any form of community work brings with it new tensions between organisational priorities and providing ground-level needs-led work.

Conclusion

The direct link between individual Sunday schools and the institutional church was only fully implemented almost a century into the movement and seems to have marked its fate. In the 1960s and the surrounding years many people chose to dissociate themselves from institutional Christianity, becoming residual believers whose faith was not active enough to be passed through the generations. This meant the church lost its institutional authority and ability to provide a framework for people's lives, but it largely failed to become more reflexive to the changing culture. Sunday schools might have survived if they had been free from the pressures of both the institutional unions and their affiliated churches and instead had adapted to the needs of the young people whom they were created to serve. The move to family church could be seen to mark the final and largest step towards catering for church needs over the needs of the young people. Those working as Christians with children and young people today need to be adaptive to the needs of the young and not their institutional authorities if they hope to engage and maintain them in a society where children are not sent but have the agency to choose to attend. The shifting role from Sunday school teacher to youth worker may evidence a change, with one of the characteristics distinguishing informal education from formal education, being its focus on the needs of the learner and its lack of pre-defined curriculum (Jeffs and Smith, 2005). A rigid institutionalism contributed to the downfall of Sunday schools and increasingly to the Christian church in general. Flexibility needs to be established if the church is to continue to engage with young people into the future. A deinstitutionalisation of Church and Christianity is needed if the church hopes to engage with a new generation. The lessons to be learned are not about how to succeed in converting young people or filling churches with a new generation of members, but about how appropriately and sensitively to engage with young people in an empowering way that inspires their critical thought. In the current 'number-crunching' culture, these are lessons deserving attention from those working with young people in general, be it with an agenda of religious education, of citizenship, or of health education.

References

BBC (2008) *How Sunday school shaped Britain*, Wednesday 2 July 2008, http//news.bbc.co.uk/1/hi/magazine/7484282.stm, last accessed 1/3/2010.

Bebbington, D.W. (1989) *Evangelicalism in Modern Britain, A History from the 1730s to the 1980s*, London, Unwin Hyman.

Brierley, D. (2003) *Joined Up, An Introduction to Youthwork and Ministry*, Cumbria, Spring Harvest Publishing/Authentic Lifestyle.

Brierley, P. (2006) *Pulling out of the Nosedive: A Contemporary Picture of Churchgoing*, London, Christian Research.

Brown, C. G. (2001) *The Death of Christian Britain*, London, Routledge.

Church of England (1996) *Youth A Part, Young People and the Church*, London, Church House Publishing.

Clayton, M.A. and Stanton, N. (2008) 'The Changing World's View of Christian Youth Work',. *Youth & Policy*, 100: 109–28.

Cliff, P.B. (1986) *The Rise and Development of the Sunday School Movement in England 1780–1980*, Surrey, National Christian Education Council.

Davie, G. (1994) *Religion in Britain since 1945, Believing Without Belonging*, Oxford, Blackwell Publishers.

Francis, L.J., Gibson, H.M. and Lankshear, D.W. (1991) The Influence of Protestant Sunday Schools on Attitudes Towards Christianity Among 11–15 Year Olds in Scotland, *British Journal of Religious Education*, 14, 35–42.

Griffiths, M. (2009) *One Generation from Extinction, How The Church Connects With The Unchurched Child*, Oxford, Monarch Books.

Hamilton, H.A. (1963) *The Family Church in Principle and Practice*, Surrey, The Religious Education Press.

Jeffs, T. and Smith, M.K. (2005) *Informal education – Conversation, Democracy and Learning (revised edition)*, Nottingham, Educational Heretics Press.

Leeds Youth Cell Network (2008) Promotional Leaflet. Leeds, LYCN.

Loukes, H. (1961) *Teenage Religion*, London, SCM Press Ltd.

McLeod, H. (2007) *The Religious Crisis of the 1960s*, Oxford, Oxford University Press.

McLeod, H. (2007a) Sport and the English Sunday School, 1869–1939. in S. Orchard and J. H. Y. Briggs (eds.) *The Sunday School Movement, Studies in the Growth and Decline of Sunday Schools* Milton Keynes, Paternoster.

Orchard, S. (2007) Sunday Schools, Some Reflections. in S. Orchard and J. H. Y. Briggs (eds.) *The Sunday School Movement, Studies in the Growth and Decline of Sunday Schools*. Milton Keynes, Paternoster.

Parsons, G. (1994) Introduction: Deciding How Far You Can Go. in G. Parsons (ed.) *The Growth of Religious Diversity, Britain from 1945*. London, Routledge.

Pilavachi, M. (2009) http//www.soulsurvivor.com/uk/about/church.html. Watford, Soul Survivor.

Rack, H. (1969) *Twentieth Century Spirituality*, London, Epworth Press.

Robson, G. (2007) Sir Joshua Fitch and 'The Sunday School of the Future'. in S.Orchard and J.H.Y. Briggs (eds.) *The Sunday School Movement, Studies in the Growth and Decline of Sunday Schools*, Milton Keynes, Paternoster.

Rosman, D. (2007) Sunday Schools and Social Change in the Twentieth Century. in S. Orchard and J.H.Y. Briggs (eds.) *The Sunday School Movement, Studies in the Growth and Decline of Sunday Schools*, Milton Keynes, Paternoster.

Savage, S., Collins-Mayo, S., Mayo, B. and Cray, G. (2006) *Making Sense of Generation Y: The Worldview Of 15–25 Year Olds*, London, Church House Publishing.

Soul Survivor (2009) http//www.soulsurvivor.com/uk/blog/. Watford, Soul Survivor.

Sutcliffe, J. (Ed.) (2001) *Tuesday's Child, A Reader for Christian Educators*, Birmingham, Christian Education Publications.

Yeo, S. (1976) *Religion and Voluntary Organisations in Crisis*, London, Croom Helm.

Primary Sources

Birmingham Council of Christian Education, Council Minutes Feb 1961–Jun 1969 *Local Christian Education Councils and Sunday School Unions, Section B, Birmingham No.8*, Birmingham University – Special Collections.

Birmingham Sunday School Union, Annual General Meetings Oct 1955–Oct 1971 *Local Christian Education Councils and Sunday School Unions, Section B, Birmingham No.14*, Birmingham University – Special Collections.

Birmingham Sunday School Union, Monthly Record, Jan 1905–Dec 1908. *Local Christian Education Councils and Sunday School Unions, Section B, Birmingham No. 33*, Birmingham University – Special Collections.

Birmingham Sunday School Union, Monthly Record, Jan 1909–Dec 1912. *Local Christian Education Councils and Sunday School Unions, Section B, Birmingham No. 34*, Birmingham University – Special Collections.

Birmingham Sunday School Union, 'News' Nos. 20–57 (excluding No. 29), Aug 1954–Nov 1963. *Local Christian Education Councils and Sunday School Unions, Section B, Birmingham No. 38*, Birmingham University – Special Collections.

Brighton and District Sunday School Union, Minutes (2001/65) Oct 1900–Dec 1911. *Local Christian Education Councils and Sunday School Unions, Section B, Brighton No.3*, Birmingham University – Special Collections.

East Herts Sunday School Union, Minutes April 1892–April 1906. *Local Christian Education Councils and Sunday School Unions, Section B, East Herts No.2*, Birmingham University – Special Collections.

East Herts Sunday School Union, Minutes Feb 1957–May 1965. *Local Christian Education Councils and Sunday School Unions, Section B, East Herts No.5*, Birmingham University – Special Collections.

CHAPTER 5

HMI Inspectorate and Youth Work, 1944–2009

Tom Wylie

Her Majesty's Inspectorate of Schools (HMI) had existed for more than a hundred years before it was asked to give some attention to youth work following the *Education Act of 1944*, which included a duty 'to promote the education of the people of England and Wales . . . and the progressive development of institutions devoted to this purpose'.[1] This general remit, stretching well beyond schools and colleges, was seen as encompassing a wide and elastic range in adult education, community associations and youth work. In this regard, the 1944 Act was building on the long-standing work of voluntary organisations, which also stretched back a hundred years through boys' and girls' clubs, Scouts and Guides, the Boys Brigade and the YMCA.

Youth work had been given salience in 1939 by Circular 1456. This seminal document, expressing a policy concern for youth welfare during wartime, urged local education authorities to set up youth committees to co-ordinate local endeavour. Looking forward to post-war reconstruction, the government had further established a national Youth Advisory Council which published *Youth Service after the War* in 1943. The 1944 Education Act reinforced this activity, but it did not use the exact term 'Youth Service' in its text choosing instead more general and ambiguous clauses to describe the work.

By 1946 a new arm of HM Inspectorate was being formed in response to the state's extended role. Specialist HMI were recruited including, in the case of youth work, those with experience in Girls' Clubs, Youth Hostels, Young Farmers and LEA youth services. Their numbers were few for the territory and range of work and one author noted the new HMI as having the characteristics of 'a missionary, an activist who would use her or his position to drive forward the intentions of the [1944] Act' (Elsdon, 2001: 27). They also brought personal qualities and temperaments. One youth work specialist had seen action with the Resistance in occupied Europe, another had been in the intelligence corps in Palestine. Such characters did not take easily to any petty bureaucracy in the Ministry or Inspectorate but in their dealings with the educational field they would contribute to what one author has described as 'the culture of the post-war Inspectorate . . . benign, optimistic, supportive. It was cautious and under-stated in its public pronouncements . . . there was an emphasis on etiquette, courtesy and collegiality . . .' (Maclure, 2000: 324).

The developmental aspect of the 1944 Act was advanced by Circular 133 of 1947 by which LEAs were expected to propose 'Schemes of FE Development', including the Youth Service. But hardly was the print dry on the legislation and HMI in post, when it became clear that the hopeful policy drive had weakened in the face of post-war austerity. In the name of economy and the need to fuel the always hungry maw of formal education, the new system anticipated by the '44 Act was generally resisted by the government of the day. Both field and Inspectorate were thus setting out to build a structure without support.

The inspection task

This constraint remained the context for youth work for much of the succeeding 60 years apart from brief periods of sunshine – the post-Albemarle Report years of the early 1960s and again early in the twenty first century as the 'Transforming Youth Work' agenda unfolded. HM Inspectors pressed on with the job, starting with a full inspection of Manchester's Youth Service in 1948. From the resulting reports it was clear that Youth Service development by local authorities remained patchy. For example London County Council had been quick to respond to the challenge of its new responsibilities but Kent, among others, relied exclusively on the voluntary sector and had no Principal Youth Officer for many years. The national Ministry declined to give any framework for local development.

In a striking internal memorandum of 1951, W.R. Elliott – later to become the Senior Chief Inspector – summarised the scene:

> The following paragraphs set out the main difficulties encountered in Youth Service, and suggest some possible ways of meeting them.
>
> 1. Ignorance of the purpose and aims of Youth Service on the part of the general public, and lack of understanding of the club technique, and lack of sympathy with young people, constitute the greatest number of problems. There is a good deal of opposition to Youth Service in the teaching profession, many members of which do not recognise youth work as a part of the educational system: where it is accepted as such it has to meet similar opposition and criticism to the 'activity' methods in schools. The low standard of work in some civic youth clubs, where everything is provided, stimulates such criticism.
>
> 2. The establishment of LEA clubs and centres which are generously staffed by untrained and in some cases inexperienced leaders, all of whom are

paid, is threatening to kill voluntary effort. It is also resulting in poor standards . . .'

(Cited in Elsdon op cit., 105)

Although Elliott's memorandum resulted in a few immediate initiatives, it was several years before his judgment bore fruit in any substantial action on policy. However this kind of memorandum also exemplifies an important truth about HMI's role for much of the post-war period; its key duty was to advise national government. Inspection visits and reports may have been helpful to those inspected; isolated local authority or voluntary sector officers may have benefited from wise counsel or at least a sympathetic ear; individual HMI may have derived pleasure from these tasks or from visiting to assess and encourage different youth units in their immense territorial Divisions, but their prime duty was to enable the Minister and civil servants in Whitehall to know what was happening across the country, the better to shape national policies or allocate scarce resources such as grant aid to voluntary organisations. 'Face the centre' was the stern injunction later given to all HMI by an astringent Senior Chief Inspector. And 'facing the centre' had to be based on evidence of work seen, not just HMI's opinion. Evidence was found through inspection, sometimes in an extensive 'full inspection' of a unit or area; more commonly through less formal 'pastoral' visits which resulted only in a note for the Ministry or for the file. At the heart of HMI practice, indeed of its belief system, was observation of, and judgement about, direct work with young people in the multifarious settings of youth work. Some HMI writing in these years had a lyricism which became unfashionable, even if the insights of later writing would often remain as compelling:

The boys are loyal to their club, but within its walls, perhaps because they are left largely to their own devices, their behaviour is sometimes more boisterous than is desirable . . . the reasons: there is no trained warden, the absence of a planned programme, and the fact that boys are called upon to play so little part in running the club.

(HMI, 1954)

To the visitor, the members presented a picture of vigorous rather than oriented life. They moved like quick-silver about the building anxious, it sometimes seemed, to find a focus of activity and not over anxious to become that focus themselves. The girls were especially mobile. There seemed little inclination to stay long at anything.

(HMI, 1964)

Following inspection visits the verbal reports by HMI to governing bodies were usually even more forthright. Those responsible for the governance of the latter club mentioned above were told 'much inventive thinking went into devising activities but few took part in them and the standard of performance was low eg. half-a-dozen boys practised PE but in their outdoor clothes' (HMI, 1964). Over time, the inspection reporting of HMI changed from such fine-grained analysis of youth work practice in individual units into more general surveys of youth provision or of the supporting infrastructure such as training. These kinds of reports could be used, often obliquely, to comment on, and thus help to shape, national programmes and policies. Although there was an increasing use of data, too rarely was HMI willing to be drawn on whether there was 'sufficient' youth work in any area: the focus remained on the quality of what was offered rather than its volume.

Three landmark events

Three landmarks dominate the Inspectorate's post-war territory: the Albemarle Report of 1960; the decision to publish HMI Reports in 1982; and the establishment of Ofsted a decade later.

Only Albemarle (Ministry of Education, 1960) was directly concerned with youth work. It set in train the substantial development of youth services which had not taken place following the 1944 Act. HMI's role was fundamental in shaping this report by supplying the evidence from inspection and by acting as the secretariat to the Albermarle Committee. The Inspectorate's own present and future role was identified in the report and HMI was thereby significant in taking forward the key recommendations. HMI assessed grants for new buildings; seconded Ted Sidebottom to head the new National College for the Training of Youth Leaders; identified and described innovative practice; and ran national courses which helped to create the basis for a reinvigorated youth service. It inspected the work which Albemarle had done so much to bring to life in a series of specific reports on different youth work units and themes. However such reports, although available to the Ministry (later Department) and to the governing body of the unit inspected, were not published. In the early 1980s this 'secret garden' was opened to all. Sir Keith Joseph, the Secretary of State for Education, believed in a greater role for the market in constructing educational provision and saw informed consumers, i.e. parents, as a necessary pre-condition of a successful market. To ensure that they would be better informed, he decided that with effect from January 1983, the reports made by HMI would be published.

Youth work publication came in on the coat tails of this schools-oriented decision. Youth work was also gaining in importance as a consequence of a growing 'moral panic' about rising youth unemployment and inner city disturbances. Youth work HMIs seemed to be well-informed reporters and youth work itself well-placed to intervene. Moreover, the Thompson Report (1982) had revived local and national policy interest in youth service provision. HMIs, notably through Edwin Sims, had been engaged with Thompson behind the scenes the same as they had been with Albemarle. These factors opened the door to the contribution of HMIs being better valued nationally. In consequence, the specialist HMI youth team was increased in number to a dozen people and diversified further in its gender and ethnicity though each still had other inspectorate duties as well as youth work.

There was no prospect of HMI ever providing published reports of all schools, still less of all youth projects. Accordingly, the national youth team decided it was not worthwhile to concentrate on publications about individual youth centres or projects. Instead it deployed its limited resources on inspecting and reporting on the overall Youth Service provision made by a particular LEA, or by a national voluntary organisation, or by inspecting a specific form of youth work, such as detached work. These reports – over 50 of them by the end of the 1980s – still based their judgments on work observed by HMI in particular clubs or projects. However, by working in larger, cross-divisional teams, it was hoped to better inform policy, assess field initiatives more effectively, and disseminate good practice more widely. Inspection also examined training, especially initial qualifying training for professional youth and community work, which resulted in a series of published reports on individual HE courses, including those at Westhill and the then Manchester Polytechnic.

During this decade HMI reported on youth work in a mushrooming variety of settings and projects, in the voluntary as well as the maintained sector. Such inspection activities challenged, widened, and deepened inspection methodology: how were judgments to be reached on street-based youth work or outdoor education, on crime prevention programmes or the totality of an authority's youth provision? The honing of collective judgments and a greater measure of 'inter-rater reliability' between different inspectors became imperative, as reports were now public documents and open to critical comment. In the days before they codified their criteria for judgment and made them publicly explicit, the strength of HMI's approach lay in internal collegiality and the testing out of perceptions and judgments with colleagues who brought a range of nation-wide inspection experience into the evaluation of a service or of a particular area of work. Nevertheless it still represented something of the tradition of a connoisseur making a judgment, albeit one refined through wide experience and challenge from one's peers; it rarely made much use of whatever data existed.

The growing diversification of youth work across the country, and its targeting of specific groups of young people according to their needs, was captured in a series of published reports. These included a seminal report on *Effective Youth Work* (1987) in the HMI series *Education Observed* which sought to characterise the distinctive values and educational methods of youth work. The report emphasised personal and social development as its principal *raison d'être* and, in case studies, exemplified how various activities could be used to this end. More specifically, there were reports on Youth Service provision by various local authorities including Wigan and Brent; on the nationwide work of Young Farmers' Clubs and Boys' Clubs; on detached youth work in Sheffield; on how youth work was responding nationwide to unemployment; and more controversially, to the needs of girls and young women. Not all of these reports passed straightforwardly into publication through the Inspectorate's editorial command. Some senior colleagues, with FE college backgrounds for example, found it difficult to comprehend how and why HMI were reporting in *Responsive Youth Work* (1990) and the various reports on the work of an education service with young prostitutes or young drug users. But all specialist reports made it into print, albeit occasionally with tempered messages. Not all brought welcome news for national government. The role of HMI as 'assessor' to the variety of national (and some international) youth bodies had long offered opportunities for gathering material about the sector and exerting influence on it. Such a role extended beyond being a message-carrier to and from the Department but also allowed the judicious deployment of HMI skills in questioning, conceptualising and persuasion, particularly in encouraging bodies to innovate to meet new needs.

Reporting independently and drawing the experience of field practice vigorously into the closed circles of government, could result in a whiff of cordite being in the atmosphere during discussions between departmental officials and HMI. Yet there were also positive initiatives as when HMI inspired Ministers to create an 'apprenticeship' scheme to bring younger, indigenous people into jobs in urban areas and offer them associated training to qualify them as professional youth workers. Some officials were open to the possibilities of developing imaginative programmes of grant aid to support and improve the youth sector. Similarly, some national voluntary organisations and local authorities could be persuaded to adjust their approaches, though Liverpool city council, at the time under the sway of Militant Tendency, rejected an HMI-inspired initiative to bring much needed cash to develop the city's youth service following civil disturbances.

By the early 1990s the Conservatives, now under John Major, were in search of a new 'big idea'. This was to be the 'Citizens' Charter' – a drive for improvement in public services, including meeting continued concern about educational standards in schools which HMI public reporting had illuminated. The new task was to create an inspection system which would reflect greater reporting responsibilities towards parents as well as to the Secretary of State, and which would inspect all (25,000) schools in a more systematic way than the relatively few HMI could achieve. Inspection would be expected to undertake more of a regulatory function. Following its return to office in the 1992 General Election, the government moved quickly to enact a new system of inspection, conspicuously independent of the

Department of Education (and of local authorities). The number of HMI would be halved but a whole new workforce of contracted inspectors created to inspect schools on a defined cycle of visits, initially every four years. The new national inspectorate, eventually named the Office for Standards in Education (Ofsted) would be much reduced and deal primarily with establishing and monitoring the new system of school inspection while half of those HMI inspecting in Further and Higher Education could transfer to the respective funding councils. Youth work, curiously, stayed with Ofsted, though only a handful of specialist youth HMI remained within this new body on its creation.

The operational approach of Ofsted for school inspection – the use of contracted external inspectors, trained and lightly supervised by HMI – did not apply to youth work inspections. The few remaining specialist HMI could no longer mount a significant inspection programme of youth provision: another approach was needed, at least initially. Youth work inspection diminished but did not disappear entirely and it benefited from two inter-related features. In common with the inspection arrangements for other sectors, an Inspection Handbook was published. This Handbook – regularly revised thereafter – set out the framework for inspection and the specific criteria HMI used in judging performance and standards of provision and management. Versions of this for youth work had existed internally since 1955 but this was its first codification and publication. Moreover, and arguably less beneficial, was the use of graded assessments of all educational provision which were seen by some as representing a consumerist political culture and may also have led to rather stark judgments about the youth provison made by local authorities. The second useful feature, once a more systematic pattern of youth work inspection was re-instated, was the employment by Ofsted of occasional or additional inspectors drawn from field positions to make up week-long inspection teams led by HMI. These two features – the Handbook and the use of inspectors drawn from the field – did much to introduce a more rigorous approach to self-evaluation by local youth services and hence to lift their standards. 'Improvement through inspection' became the slogan and the combination of external and internal evaluation bore fruit. In time, a rolling programme of Ofsted inspections of all (150) local authority youth services was completed and a national report on the youth work secured within them was published in 2009 (Ofsted, 2009). There was also some complementary work, as before, on assessing national voluntary youth organisations in the context of the DFES national grant pro- grammes, but this was considerably reduced in the Ofsted era and eventually disappeared. Moreover, HMI were rarely able to mount the thematic national surveys of different forms of youth work which had been such a feature of the 1980s. A significant change also took shape in the policy relationship with the Department which was no longer as intimate as it had been in the decades before

Ofsted's creation and the consequent physical and emotional separation from Departmental officials and ministers. In any case, the approach to policy-making by government had altered markedly from the more leisured and consensual days of the Albemarle Report and even of Thompson. HMI had become but one of a number of influences on the national scene and ministers tended to rely more on hand-picked special advisers or think-tanks, while the ever-changing raft of ministers and civil servants soon lost any sense of historic policy development and indeed of the nature of the youth sector.

Notwithstanding these factors, it was a notable achievement for the small but determined HMI team of specialists to maintain any inspection focus on youth work in the turbulent world of ever-changing structures – within Ofsted itself but also in the creation first of the Connexions service and, eventually, the wholesale reconstruction of local education authorities into Children's Services from 2005.This structural shift was also accompanied by a more explicit regulatory purpose for all the inspectorates of public services and a more overt focus on standards of performance within them. Reports on local authority youth services remained freestanding until the national cycle was completed and these also contributed to assessments by multi-disciplinary Inspection teams of the whole children's services of an authority. These assessments became increasingly reliant on data rather than the observation of practice. Nevertheless, although the evidence became more attenuated, the particular specialism of youth work continued to have a place – and visibility – both in reports on individual local authorities now with their wider responsibilities for the young, and also in occasional national documents summarising the issues and trends in youth work itself as identified through inspection. The most recent, published in 2009, noted the improving effectiveness of local authority youth services but commented that 'many local authorities, elected members and communities held unrealistic expectations of what youth services could achieve with the resources available' (Ofsted, 2009). Such reports despite their cogent analysis and expression could not by themselves secure a consistent valuing of youth work's contribution to the lives of young people in the new structures. In this regard youth work had to compete against the pressures of other services, with different approaches and values which often emphasised the safeguarding or guidance of the young rather than their development..

Conclusion

One of the lessons to be drawn from the shaping of educational policy in the second half of the twentieth century is that all policies are interim and incomplete.

(Maclure, 2000: 331)

This was certainly the case for youth work and for its inspection. No one doubted that schools and colleges should exist, and be resourced. This was rarely true for youth work. In such a context, successive generations of HMI saw it as their duty not just to seek to inspect independently and objectively but also to advocate for a form of work which was frequently under political, administrative or financial pressure and sometimes under attack. Idealism about the purposes and values of youth work often had to be blended with realism, even disappointment, about some of its practice and about the continued absence of a sustained political will which would even out the wide disparities in local provision. In the absence of this commitment, one of HMI's roles was to reinforce youth workers' sense of their own worth and of the validity of their chosen vocation. They did this through personal contact at many levels; through advice to individuals or through running national courses; through seeking to edge policy and practice forward as assessors to various bodies across the rich diversity of youth provision and in more formal advice to officials and Ministers. Publications could help to clarify purposes as well as to report judgments but the bedrock remained the insightful observation of youth work practice. HM Inspectors who reported on youth work were always few in number and they had no power beyond a right of access. Their influence on national policy ebbed and flowed but in their local endeavours, they sought to bear in mind the first instructions given to HMI in 1840: 'Inspection is not intended as a means of exercising control, but of offering assistance'. It was an appropriate spirit in which to approach the task of inspecting youth work – a form of educational practice which conceives itself to be in a similar relationship with the young.

Note

1   This paper describes arrangements in England. Although both governmental and inspectorate policies and structures differed in the other UK jurisdictions a similar approach to the role of inspecting youth work was adopted by their inspectorates, at least until the creation of Ofsted.

References

Elsdon, K.T. (2001) *An education for the people? A History of HMI and Lifelong learning 1944–1992* Leicester,NIACE.

HM Inspectorate: (1954) *Litherland Boys Club*, Lancs, unpublished.

—— (1964) *Victory Youth Club*, Garston, Liverpool, unpublished.

—— (1987) *Effective Youth Work*, London, Dept of Education and Science.

—— (1990) *Responsive Youth Work*, London, HMSO.

Maclure, S. (2001) *The Inspectors' Calling – HMI and The Shaping of Educational Policy 1945–1992*, London, Hodder and Stoughton.

Ministry of Education (1943) *Youth Service After the War*. London, HMSO.

Ministry of Education (1944) *Education Act 1944*. London, HMSO.

Ministry of Education (1947) *Schemes of Further Education, Circular 133*. London, HMSO.

Ministry of Education (1960) *The Youth Service in England and Wales*, (The Albemarle Report) London, HMSO.

Office for Standards in Education (Ofsted) (2009) *Engaging Young People: Local Authority Youth Work*, London.

The Thompson Report (1982) *Experience and Participation*, London, HMSO.

CHAPTER 6

Anomalous Identities, Youth Work Amidst 'Trashy Daydreams' and 'Monstrous Nightmares'[1]

Simon Bradford

This chapter explores tensions in the professionalisation of youth work from the mid twentieth century (the 1940s) to the present time.

Historically youth work has been positioned at the margins of other practices and institutions, somewhere between schooling and social work. It has assumed an 'in-between-ness' that in turn, has placed youth workers (or youth *leaders* as they were in the 1940s) in an anomalous position. Cultural anomaly, '. . . an element which does not fit a given set or series . . .' (Douglas, 1966: 47–9) is invariably understood to be socially threatening or polluting in some way as it transgresses the normative categories and classifications that constitute the social bond. Tidying the world into categories and creating boundaries within the symbolic order expresses the '. . . yearning for rigidity . . . in us all' (ibid.: 200). Anomalous entities undermine boundaries and the security they confer. Social responses to anomaly may be to ignore, to condemn or to attempt to re-define the anomaly in new or familiar terms in order to manage the contradictions implied by its presence. Thus, as well as being troublesome, anomaly might be an important driver of change. Youth workers can be understood as historically anomalous, fitting neither one occupational category nor another (neither teacher nor social worker). Youth work is a marginal and 'borderland' practice and this has made its attempts to become acknowledged as a profession and to sustain a professional identity intensely problematic. Youth work's twentieth century history (from the second world war onwards) exposes this anomalous status, which is reflected in its current position within integrated services for young people.

During the 1940s, and as part of the wartime need to manage population (Bradford, 2006) a network of professional training for those seeking a career in youth work was established in six universities under Circular 1598 (Board of

Education, 1942). Although going some way in establishing the idea that youth work necessarily relied on a formal body of knowledge and skill acquired through university-based training, its professional status remained relatively marginal until the early 1960s. However, the establishment of the National College for the Training of Youth Leaders, following publication of the Albemarle Report in 1960 (Ministry of Education, 1960) revitalised youth work's professional claim.

The chapter argues that youth work's mid-twentieth-century identity can be understood in terms of an influential *expressive* discourse existing in tension with growing demands for *instrumental* practice, and reflecting deeper social structural dynamics. Modernity (as capitalism) can be understood as encompassing both symbolic (expressive) and technical-industrial (instrumental) dimensions. In a specialised division of labour, personal experience (and the self) is fragmented, torn between the demands of impersonal institutional structures and the private sphere. Bernice Martin suggests that relative affluence (generated through the instrumentalism of the technical-industrial order) released people from the imperatives of survival to 'discover' a whole range of 'expressive needs', characteristically fulfilled in the apparently authentic domains of private and personal life which held '. . . a mirror to the egoistic and anomic normality of modern society' (Martin, 1981: 17). Thus, a pervasive romantic and expressive individualism (asserting the pre-eminence of the self and the importance of individual, especially emotional, experience) became part of the cultural script of northern European modernity. Its ethos was influential and has persisted in youth work's occupational cultures especially in the celebration of personal growth and learning from experience. It was exemplified in youth work discourse by the influential *Experience and Participation* (DES, 1982) which codified this worldview. By the 1990s, however, the increasing influence of neo-liberal economics in the UK signalled new demands for 'value for money' and clear practices and structures of managerial accountability (e.g. Maychell et al., 1996). This created discord between these worldviews. These tensions are ongoing and manifested in growing demands for instrumentalised practices in present-day integrated services designed to manage and audit youth transitions (Bradford, 2005) leading to contestation over the authentic social role of youth work and youth workers and culminating in *In Defence of Youth Work* (IDYW).[2] The IDYW campaign's (essentially expressive and romantic) principles are clearly outlined in the open letter that was circulated in 2009. Its position is exemplified by a commitment to '. . . valuing and attending to the here-and-now of young people's experience rather than just focusing on 'transitions' . . . [and to] . . . conversations with young people which start from their concerns and within which both youth worker and young person are educated and out of which opportunities for new learning and experience can be created' (IDYW, 2010). IDYW is, of course, not the first time that institutional challenges have been posed to instrumentalism (for example, the youth worker trade unions have constantly argued an expressive worldview) and there has been a strong expressive current in youth work's professional cultures since the 1940s. However, IDYW's importance lies in its 'single-issue' stance (revitalising a specific kind of youth work), clear expression of a specific and resistant position and its wider reflection of a perceived crisis in neo-liberalism (Brie, 2009). This chapter offers an account of the broader historical context in which these matters arose.

Real or illusory professionals?

Despite earlier aspirations that youth work would contribute to the development of the young 'earner' as young 'learner' (Board of Education, 1941: 18) a sense of bleakness characterises accounts of youth work in the post-war years. Ministry of Education Annual Reports through the 1950s make gloomy reading (eg. Ministry of Education 1953: 21, and Ministry of Education, 1954: 30). Schools were expected to take on a new role in the 'moral regeneration' of the nation, and educational priorities lay in technical education contributing to economic output (Lowe, 1988: 18; Tinkler, 2001). Until the end of the 1950s, National Service absorbed substantial numbers of young men and provided them with character-building experiences, rather like a surrogate youth service (Matthewson, 1961: 166). State indifference towards youth work was evident throughout this period. Perhaps surprisingly, however, questions about the professional training of youth leaders (of whom, probably about 400–500 were employed at that time in England and Wales) remained on the education agenda until the early 1950s. Three significant Government committees reported on youth work training at this time: McNair, Jackson and Fletcher (Board of Education, 1944; Ministry of Education, 1949; and Ministry of Education, 1951).

Analysis of Board and Ministry of Education records illustrates a recurrent paradox that has continued to position youth work as anomalous, 'betwixt and between' (Turner, 1997). This concerns the value implicitly acknowledged (by the state, youth workers themselves, or educators for example) of youth work's 'flexibility' and 'fluidity', yet, and perhaps as a consequence, a concurrent uncertainty about its precise nature and purpose and the form that the training of its personnel should take. Whilst the need for youth workers and the value of youth work as '. . . an integral part of the public system of education' (Board of Education, 1944: 96) was repeatedly invoked, it was also challenged, particularly after the McNair Report's publication in 1944. For example, in an internal paper summarising the views of HMI on McNair's proposals for the professional training of youth leaders, Miles-Davies (an Assistant Principal in the Board of Education) was able to '. . . confess to one or two private convictions':

*The technique of youth leadership, such as it is, is something which should be given in small doses and by stealth in the course of a general education. Thus I have a bias against **long** 'youth' courses . . . and prefer the notion of . . . short courses of technique and experience (for) students who are themselves engaged in a university or similar course of general education. I am in fact a bit bothered by the youth leader specially and mysteriously trained, and indeed I don't over much care for the title 'Youth Leader' anyway.*

(Youth Service Inspectors Advisory Committee, 1944: 4)

Miles-Davies' ambivalence about professional youth workers, shared in the Board and, subsequently, in the Ministry, can be gauged from another memorandum written to Sir Robert Wood, Deputy Secretary at the Board of Education from 1940 until 1946, some 12 months later. This pointed out that,

. . . [in the] immediate future there is likely to be a considerable development of work in this social-cum-educational field . . . There is no doubt in my mind that a real danger is involved in our widening the social services without at the same time taking steps to ensure a supply of trained social leaders.

(Miles-Davies, 1945)

These suggest concurrent uncertainty, scepticism and in some ways a perverse ambivalence about youth work and training that goes some way to account for its limited success in sharpening claims to a professional identity in the 1940s and early 1950s. However, in the absence of state interest at this time, the professionalisation of youth work remained unrealised.

Ambiguity of a different kind characterised the three committees that reported on the training of youth leaders between 1944 and 1951. Questions about youth work's status as an authentic career choice emerged in all three reports. Despite developments during the war years, youth work was largely understood (other than by the youth leaders themselves) as a temporary occupation that might attract recruits from teaching or allied occupations. McNair for example, believed that it was realistic to think of the youth leader's average working life as 15 or 20 years, because of the 'great physical demands' of the work (Board of Education, 1944: 99). This argument was cited in the Jackson Report in 1949 with an added dimension. Because youth work was predominantly evening work, '. . . leaders tend to be cut off from the normal leisure interests of their contemporaries . . . (and) this is bad both for the leaders and the young people in their clubs' (Ministry of Education, 1949: 3). For Jackson, it was unlikely that youth leaders would work beyond the age of 35.

In contrast, in 1951 the National Advisory Council on the Training and Supply of Teachers (chaired by Professor B.A. Fletcher, responsible for the Circular 1598

Course at Bristol University in 1942) asserted that some entrants might choose youth work as a life-long career. Short-term involvement in Youth Service by teachers, or a move from Youth Service to '. . . a post in one of the growing series of occupations that require an experience of both educational and social work' were also acknowledged (Ministry of Education, 1951: 5–6) and transferability between youth work and related occupations (particularly teaching) was discussed. Jackson, for example, argued that youth work should be organised as an integral part of the wider education service, with opportunities for movement '. . . from one branch to another and which, as a whole, offers prospects of a developing career' (Ministry of Education, 1949: 3). The view that youth work was temporary rather than a 'career for life', a form of career break for teachers, or experience for other work in the human services partially undermined the claim that youth work had a distinct underlying body of knowledge and skill that warranted its classification as a profession. This is a view of youth work as 'in-between', neither entirely located in one occupational space nor the other. The imprecise location of youth work and youth workers as *liminal* and '. . . neither here nor there' (Turner: 95) poses a challenge to a stratified occupational order and attracts potential hostility from its interlocutors. Despite this, each of the reports asserted youth work's *professional* identity, and each made proposals for the specialised training of professional youth leaders. Elements of social science, social administration, and practical areas like group work and health education were included. All three reports distinguished between theory and practical work, although neither Jackson nor Fletcher indicated how much of each should be included, their outcomes, or how each could be assessed. All three reports shared the view that practice knowledge should be framed in terms of instrumental discourse, with elements of a liberal curriculum added in the Fletcher report. However, by 1953 only one of the Circular 1598 university-based courses remained, at University College Swansea.

Albemarle: deploying the 'power of leadership'

Post-war reconstruction and the expanding welfare state led to growth in the technical and semi-professional sectors of the British economy. This included professionalisation of the service occupations (social work, therapists, health workers and so on). The characteristic strategy of these occupations was to achieve professional status (a form of social closure) by emulating the traditional professions of law and medicine, defining a specific expertise that could be tested by the acquisition of formal qualifications, typically in a university (Perkin, 1989: 439). As the powerful partner, the state facilitated professional recognition, as professionalism was essential to realising the ideal of social progress embodied in the post-war welfare state (Johnson, 1993: 150–1). Although a distinctive expertise had eluded youth work in the 1940s, social well-being and the quality of life became legitimate and desirable goals of the human service occupations in post-war Britain. The helping occupations (including youth work) developed '. . . a professional rhetoric which presented them as servants in the cause of expressive enrichment . . .' obscuring their social control functions whilst investing in them a morally uplifting purpose (Martin, 1981: 196). This invariably emphasised aspects of personal development and self-realisation. However, these occupations retained (and retain) a contradictory core of instrumental *and* expressive imperatives, the source of tension both within the occupations themselves. Indeed, the emergence of IDYW is indicative of this.

The Albemarle Committee was appointed in 1958 by the Secretary of State to report on the condition of the Youth Service in England and Wales. The appearance of a distinctive youth culture in the context of shifting authority relations, changing patterns of work and consumption, and predictions of a demographic 'bulge' in the youth population meant the committee's work assumed considerable urgency. For Albemarle, the Youth Service's poor state occurred as a consequence of employing insufficient numbers of skilled workers. Echoing McNair's 1944 recommendations, Albemarle affirmed that placing the service on a firm *professional* footing with '. . . a sufficient body of full-time leaders, trained for the job . . .' (Ministry of Education, 1960: 71) would release the 'power of leadership' to influence young people's lives and the Committee argued for salary scales and pension arrangements for youth workers to be improved.

Like Jackson in 1949, Albemarle suggested that qualified teachers would provide the main source of recruitment to youth work, with social workers and 'mature persons with a natural gift for leadership' adding to this (Ministry of Education, 1960: 72). However, unlike McNair, Jackson or Fletcher, Government accepted Albemarle's recommendations, which led to an expansion of youth work and significant developments in training. Albemarle proposed that the number of full-time youth leaders should rise from 700 (in 1960) to 1300 by 1966, and that an 'emergency training college' was needed to increase numbers. The National College for the Training of Youth Leaders was established at Leicester in 1961, offering one-year full-time courses leading to the award of a Diploma in Youth Work between 1961 until 1970. More than 1000 students completed these courses in the period.

Youth work's 'New Romantics': Albemarle inspired training

During the ten-year life of the National College a new repertoire of techniques and practices developed in the training of professional youth workers. Publications by

National College staff during the late 1960s and 1970s formed the youth work canon and the College's practices soon became the orthodoxy in youth work training and, indeed, in youth work practice. There was some sense in the field that those who had trained at the College were an elite. Critics of the College's intellectual legacy suggested that it exercised '. . . a disproportionate influence on youth work training for both full and part-time workers during the following decades' (Jeffs and Smith, 1993: 14). The College's approach was paradigmatic, dominating youth work training throughout the 1960s and 1970s with its underlying account of liberal youth work, moderated later by more radicalised discourses (Bradford, 2004: 247) that shaped the Youth Service from practitioner, managerial and academic positions. Following its incorporation by Leicester Polytechnic in 1971, some of the College's staff went to other higher education institutions where their ideas were disseminated through newly established professional training courses that proliferated in the 1970s. Arguably, the College's influence, especially its humanistic and expressive aspects, has persisted into the 2000s.

The National College's work constituted a departure from earlier practices of youth worker training. No longer, for example, was knowledge disseminated as neutral or objective information as in the Circular 1598 courses in the 1940s. Rather, the value of knowledge was determined by the extent to which it could be grounded in the *student's own* experience. Reflecting on students' engagement with the 'human sciences' two prominent members of the College's staff suggested that:

> . . . *general principles observed in human growth and development relate to **his own** past and current development and behaviour; the general concepts devised to describe the social interaction of one human being with another refer to **his own** relationships with other people; the general patterns which have been described in past and contemporary societies make up the background against which to see **his own** life.*
>
> (Davies and Gibson, 1967: 190. My emphases)

This incipient student centred pedagogy reflected a wider discourse exemplified in a combination of Rogerian and Rousseauian ideas of an individualised personhood to be achieved through experiential learning. Personal experience became the guarantor of knowledge's authenticity and the key to the development of the self, construed as both precursor and effect of these practices. Rogers, for example, had urged that the individual should strive to identify his 'true' self, value the immediacy and authenticity of the 'open' relationship with others, cherish the feelings which emanate from this, and constantly seek further opportunities to 'take responsibility' for self-development (Rogers, 1967). This cultivated engagement with knowledge construction characterised the National College's approach to the professional formation of youth workers.

National College academics had a clear sense of the professional persona, the transformations and identifications to be encouraged in the self of the novice youth workers for whom they were responsible. In a statement of principle and policy, the College's intended outcomes for students were carefully outlined:

> . . . *[they should] know how to help young people use the experience of group membership to further their own development . . . (and) be able to make and use purposeful relationships with young people as individuals and in groups*
> . . .

> (National College for the Training of Youth Leaders, 1966: 3)

Moreover, it meant that,

> . . . *[to help] young people to grow up successfully . . . (the worker) needs to be a person who has himself succeeded in achieving a fair measure of maturity and developing a good many of his own potentialities; who, without being complacent, accepts himself as he is and is able to continue to grow.*

> (Ibid.: 3)

The work of the National College was based on broadly humanistic and romantic assumptions of personhood (in the young person with whom youth workers would operate and, importantly, the youth workers themselves). Romantic individualism entails the belief that individual mind, feelings, sentiments and experience offer a primary source of truth and a guide to conduct, regardless of external social constraints and conventions. This view had already started to influence social work and youth work training in the late 1940s (Bradford, 2007) and the acquisition of abstract or technocratic knowledge (derived from the social sciences, for example) was becoming secondary. The 'person' was regarded as central to the professional enterprise and had privileged status in this form of training. One of the assumptions underlying National College courses was outlined by one of its academics; '. . . the **personal development** of the student was as important as his acquisition of particular knowledge and skills needed for the work . . .' (Watkins, 1971: 7, original emphasis).

Since its inception in the nineteenth century youth work's task had been to cultivate the self-regulating, responsible and autonomous young person. Following Albemarle, humanistic discourse began to offer a repertoire of concepts, ideas and a vocabulary in which to imagine young people in a way that made them amenable to intervention *and* to shape the professional formation of youth workers who would work with them. This discourse (embodied in human relations psychology) signalled the discovery of group dynamics and group processes (the development of norms, attitudes, patterns of communication, difference, conflict, status, and so on) and their influences on relations of psychological bonding and resistance, the formation of individual identity, self-image, and self-esteem, and the effect of these on organisation and group performance. In effect, by managing these processes, a compact between the individual and the social could be created, subsequently reflected in youth work's attempts to accommodate individual young people, their aspirations and desires, and the wider social demands made of them. This discourse and its accounts of the individual subject initiated the interrogation of a domain of being and conduct by rational (yet, also invoking *emotional*) knowledge and practices. Youth workers trained in these practices were to intervene in the lives of young people in ways that reflected their own experiences at the National College. It is not difficult to see the inherent tension between the celebration of humanistic/romantic principles and youth workers' formal regulatory role in relation to young people and their conduct. This tension has been a persistent presence in youth work (and similar occupations), recently emerging in the context of IDYW.

However, in spite of the fundamentally expressive (and, arguably, dominant) discourse shaping the College's work, youth work was simultaneously understood through the technical deployment of knowledge and skills governed by dispassionate judgement and cultivated professional neutrality. As well as privileging self-realisation and personal development, the College seems to have established a somewhat austere emotional regime. Halmos identified a similar self-discipline in the 'faith of the counsellors', the '. . . scrupulousness of self-criticism . . .' is deployed so that the counsellor avoids '. . . any kind of self-indulgence, tries not to fulfil therapeutic ambition, or refrains from exploiting his professional function for self-therapy' (Halmos, 1978: 92). In this, helping (or educating) is an activity through which the professional is expected to seek no self-gratification and to maintain appropriate distance defined by the boundaries of meticulous self-control. There is, of course, a tension between such control and the pursuit of self-expression.

Self-knowledge emerges in such regimes to establish and monitor a separation between the desires of the private self and the expectations and injunctions that form the basis of professional integrity. Writing about work with young people, Davies and Gibson suggested that self-awareness could circumvent the corruption of the professional project. Self-knowledge, they argued, entails the youth worker's deepening understanding:

> . . . of more permanently and extensively influential personal responses and, in particular, [it] can bring perspective and detachment to work in which an adult has become too deeply involved . . . Pride, need for achievement,

compensation for frustration elsewhere in life may infect his work. The altruistic purpose with which he set out in social education may become partially or wholly lost to sight, submerged, if he is not aware of his own reactions, amid a welter of compensations and personal release.

(Davies and Gibson, 1967: 189)

Self-knowledge was important in relation to the principle of 'acceptance' of both self and other. Accepting others *as they are* became an article of faith in youth work and social work in the 1960s and 1970s and a disposition that the National College sought to foster in its students. Non-judgementalism, cultivated in conduct and responses towards others became the exemplar of acceptance and the departure-point for social educational work with young people ('starting from where the young person is'). A cameo example comes from Leighton, a senior academic at the College,

The three young men who appear at the door of the club dressed in leathers, with hair reaching their shoulders, looking unsmilingly at whatever is going on are more likely to produce the thought, 'Oh dear, trouble' from a number of adults than a move which demonstrates a non-judgemental attitude . . . [the youth worker] may not approve, privately, of certain modes of dress or behaviour but he has to ask himself how his own attitudes, beliefs and values affect his demonstration of acceptance, and whether by some response, inflection of voice or facial expression he is expressing disapproval.

(Leighton, 1972: 94)

Drawing on the injunction to love one's neighbour as oneself, Matthews suggested that acceptance is not possible unless one first of all loves oneself. The worker cannot '. . . relate himself helpfully to young people unless he can accept himself as able to be of help and worthy of their response to him'. In the context of professional youth work training, the student must be helped to 'live with and love the changed image of himself which emerges' (Matthews, 1966: 108). This entails emotional labour in 'getting to know' self, in marking out its dimensions and capacities, registering its foibles, gauging its impact on others, and determining its potential for continuing transformation. As Leighton put it, youth work requires:

. . . a professional approach to the work . . . and the key factor in a professional approach is discipline . . . (the youth worker) needs a framework of reference for disciplined thinking about his work and it is against this framework that he reflects on any part or all of the work he does within his task as youth worker.

(Leighton, 1972: 191)

Leighton's text epitomises the typically calculative and 'problem-solving' nature of the instrumental aspects of the College's work. This assumes that professional work is a matter of deploying the appropriate knowledge or skill in order to resolve the problem at hand; in effect, ensuring the right fit between means and ends. As such, it contrasts with the College's expressive imperatives (and represents a further tension). This tension is retained in contemporary youth work and animates IDYW's resistance to managerialised youth work in favour of a genre that embodies democratic and emancipatory discourse.

The National College accommodated an underlying expressive discourse with an incipient technical-rationalism that characterised the training defined in McNair, Jackson and Fletcher. For example, training in social group work (imported from the USA in the late 1940s, Kuenstler, 1955: 16–7) which developed through the 1960s focused primarily on personal development, yet emphasised the need for the worker to be helped by a supervisor in '. . . checking his observations and the significance he attaches to them, (and) prompting him to be aware of the ways in which his own feelings are involved in his work' (Matthews, 1966: 25). As a senior academic at the College, Matthews' injunction suggests that this practice was characterised not only by developing the emotional domain of the self but the discipline of the novice practitioner in recognising and cultivating aspects of self that could enhance or diminish practice.

Reshaping identities in miserable times

In the 1960s and 1970s youth work became an identifiable, although ambiguous, practice (or set of practices) and was incorporated within local authorities and voluntary sector organisations. During this period, it demonstrated many of the features of increased professionalism, growing numbers of training courses in universities and polytechnics, the emergence of 'youth work academics' and a body of youth work literature, in-service training for employed workers and improvements in conditions of service being among these. Despite this, questions remained about the nature of this professionalism (Davies, 1999: 190) and a foundation for more recent developments was established. Indeed, youth work has assumed some prominence in the developing youth support services in England during the first decade of the new millennium (Davies, 2005: 3). According to the Children's Workforce Development Council there were just over 3000 professionally qualified youth workers in Local Authorities in England in 2008 (CWDC, 2009: 47) not including those in the voluntary sector. In the financial year 1957–1958, 211 full-time youth leaders were employed in local authorities and 430 in the voluntary sector in England (Ministry of Education, 1960: 119). We know little about their qualifications, but from 2010, in England, youth workers will require a minimum qualification of an honours degree in youth work. This suggests that the process of professionalisation has accelerated since the second half of the twentieth century.

The foregoing discussion delineates aspects of youth work's identity between the 1940s and 1960s. It is significant that it subsequently advanced arguments, to convince the state as gatekeeper of professionalism (Perkin, 1989: 395) to grant youth leadership professional status similar to other service occupations. The task here is to explain youth work's (relative) success in this respect; after all, it could so easily have failed to achieve any such status. Several factors are suggested.

The emergence of mass post-war youth culture generated both popular and political anxiety in Britain. The genesis and contours of the youth problem were carefully mapped in the Albemarle Report and a range of youth work interventions suggested in response, which developed a pre-existing institutional architecture. Indeed, Albemarle and youth workers succeeded, ideologically, in using mid-century social anxiety to further the professional development of youth work. Without the moral panic generated by mass youth culture (similar to concerns expressed about youth welfare during the second world war) youth work's distinctive contribution to the management of young people might have gone unrecognised. Youth work contributed to managing young people's transitions through the transitional spaces created in the mid twentieth century capitalist division of labour. Of course, the problem of youth transitions had existed previously but was seen anew in glaring media representations of young people (Davis, 1990). Shifting patterns of authority relations and an apparent decline in generational and class-based deference, demographic shifts, material affluence and new patterns of consumption (particularly among young people), the demise of national service and the unremitting rhythms of American Rock and Roll made youth worker intervention in young people's lives politically irresistible.

However, as we suggested earlier, other sociological factors contributed to creating the conditions that enabled youth work to gain recognition of its expertise and helped to confirm a degree of professional identity. The most significant of these was the developing significance of the emotional domain of the self. As Weber had pointed out in the early twentieth century, modernity was to be understood as signalling the 'disenchantment of the world' where '. . . the ultimate and most sublime values have retreated from public life either into the transcendental realm of mystic life or into the brotherliness of direct and personal human relations' (Gerth and Mills, 1967: 155). The demise of public culture in broadly secularised, rational, capitalist and liberal twentieth-century Western societies led in part to the transmutation of political concerns into individualised psychological categories and states which became the focus of governmental power (Dean, 2010: 192). Late modern *mass* society contained a tension. The instrumental demands of social existence shaped by impersonal and bureaucratic institutions resulted in individual experience becoming increasingly fragmented in a pervasive normlessness (Sennett, 1986: 263; Jenks, 2005: 181). Halmos points to the failure of political action to touch the acutely *personal* misery of modern loneliness generated through the anomie and alienation associated with mass society. One consequence is for meaning and expressive fulfilment to become located exclusively within private and personal domains, the family and, above all, in the intensely reflexive personal relationship (Giddens, 1992). Identifying the 'trashy daydreams' and 'monstrous nightmares of mechanised humanity' that haunt modern lives, Halmos points to the profound belief in contemporary Western cultures that such misery can only be assuaged in the intimate domains of the personal (1978: 21–3). It is no coincidence that the principal focus of youth work's intervention has been the personal relationship, claimed as the vehicle, *par excellence*, for achieving individual wellbeing.

During the 1960s and thereafter, youth work (and related occupations, social work, therapeutic and education practices) privileged the cultivated intimacy of the personal relationship and celebrated its capacity for individual development and expression. Youth workers' engagement with young people's development en-sured their place in the personal services that expanded through the 1960s and 1970s. The 1960s expressive revolution, set against the techno-rationality and instrumental imperatives of advanced industrial capitalism, provided a context in which to nurture techniques of the self that youth workers developed at the National College and which animated their work with young people. Personal growth and development, expressed in the therapeutic sensibility outlined by Lasch (1991: 7) and given form in Rogerian-style encounter groups had some impact on the helping professions at the time. This sensibility embodied aspects of 'anti-structure' (Turner, 1997: 112) that mirrored the liminal status of youth and, indeed, of youth work. However, the Albemarle worldview and its expression in the work of the National College contained an inevitable contradiction between its consti-tutive expressive (anti-structure) and instrumental (structure) elements. That contradiction, the cause of endless contestation about youth work's authentic place and purpose in the world, remained relatively constrained until recently.

Conclusions

This chapter has sketched youth work's mid twentieth-century history and aspects of its professionalisation since the 1940s. That occurred, substantially, through claims made for an expertise in the management of young people's personal relationships and development. This resonated with mid century resistance to the anomie and alienation of mass culture and a celebration of the imputed authenticity of the emotional and affective domains of personhood that offered refuge. In part, youth work's progress in this respect was influenced by the counter-culture of the late 1960s (as well as by incipient moral panic that focused on domestic mass youth culture in the 1950s and 60s). Broader social changes, in particular transformations associated with neo-liberalism, shaped youth work (and the public sector as a whole) in the last decades of the twentieth and the first decade of the twenty-first centuries. The strong managerialism of audit culture that colonised much of the public services in these years drew attention to youth work's apparently fuzzy rationale. However, to understand youth work solely in that way (as vague or aimless) is to misread its underlying expressive ideology and to acknowledge instrumentalism alone. The shift from expressive to instrumental ideals in public services, especially embodied in the services tasked to manage youth transitions, has exposed expressive ideology as an element in the anomalous historical identity of youth work. IDYW and its challenge to the rationality of contemporary managerialism can be seen as one outworking of this. What is interesting is the retention of the imperatives that underlay youth work's achievement of professional status through the 1960s and 1970s, in particular its expressive core. Clearly, these continue to resonate. Youth work, as I have suggested elsewhere (Bradford, 2004) has a peerless mobility and a fluidity that enables it to alter shape according to prevailing policy definitions of youth need. This is both strength and constraint as youth work is, in effect, held in a perpetual state of ambiguity with the inevitable potential of transgressing and polluting the occupational boundaries that constitute a socially coherent division of labour. However, it is through its 'shape-shifting' capacity that the sometimes-conflicting elements discussed here are likely to be accommodated. Its precise future form, and that of post-recessionary professionalism more widely, remains to be seen.

Notes

1   This is Halmos's 1970s characterisation of modernity in Western societies in which youth work emerged as a distinct social entity. In some ways, Halmos anticipates the work of Zygmunt Bauman who offers an analysis of the 'liquidity' of contemporary social life (see, for example, Bauman, 2007).

2   IDYW is a social movement initiated by youth work advocates in 2009 aiming to resist current 'managerialist' policy developments in youth work and to promote democratic, emancipatory and authentic youth work. It is organised through social networking sites, a dedicated website and regional meetings.

References

Bauman, Z. (2007) *Liquid Times, Living in an Age of Uncertainty*, Cambridge, Polity Press.
Board of Education (1941) *Education After the War*, internal Board of Education memorandum, 4 July 1941.

Board of Education (1942) *Emergency Courses of Training for those Engaging in the Youth Service*, Circular 1598, London, HMSO.

Board of Education (1944) *Teachers and Youth Leaders, (McNair Report)*, Report of the Committee Appointed by the President of the Board of Education to Consider the Supply, Recruitment and Training of Teachers and Youth Leaders, London, HMSO.

Bradford, S. (2004) 'Management of Growing Up', in Roche, J. Tucker, S. Thomson, R. and Flynn, R. (eds.) (second edition), *Youth in Society*, London, Sage Publications, 245–54.

Bradford, S. (2005) Modernising Youth Work, From The Universal to The Particular and Back Again. in Harrison, R., and Wise, C., (eds.) *Working with Young People*, London, Sage Publications, 57–69.

Bradford, S. (2006) Practising the Double Doctrine of Freedom, Managing Young People in the Context of War. in Gilchrist, R., Jeffs, T., and Spence, J., (eds) *Drawing on the Past, Studies in the History of Community and Youth Work*, Leicester, NYA.

Bradford, S. (2007) The Good Youth Leader, Constructions of Professionalism in English Youth Work. 1939–1945, *Ethics and Social Welfare*, 1: 3, 293–309.

Brie, M. (2009) Ways out of the Crisis of Neo-liberalism. *Development Dialogue*, 51, 15–31.

CWDC (2009) *A Picture Worth Millions. State of The Young People's Workforce*, Leeds, CWDC.

Davis, J. (1990) *Youth and the Condition of Britain, Images of Adolescent Conflict*, London, Athlone Press.

Davies, B., and Gibson, A. (1967) *The Social Education of the Adolescent*, London, University of London Press.

Davies, B. (1999) *From Voluntaryism to the Welfare State, A History of the Youth Service in England, Volume 1, 1939–1979*, Leicester, Youth Work Press.

Davies, B. (2005) *Youth Work, A Manifesto for Our Times*, Leicester, The National Youth Agency.

Dean, M. (2010) *Governmentality. Power and Rule in Modern Society*, London, Sage Publications.

Department of Education and Science (1982) *Experience and Participation, Report of the Review Group on the Youth Service in England and Wales*, (Cmnd 8686) London, HMSO.

Douglas, M. (1966) *Purity and Danger: An analysis of the Concept of Pollution and Taboo*, London, Routledge and Kegan Paul.

Gerth, H.H. and Wright Mills, C. (1967) *From Max Weber, Essays in Sociology*, London, Routledge and Kegan Paul.

Giddens, A. (1992) *The Transformation of Intimacy, Sexuality, Love and Eroticism in Modern Societies*, Cambridge, Polity Press.

Halmos, P. (1978) (second revised edition) *The Faith of the Counsellors*, London, Constable.

IDYW, (2010) http//indefenceofyouthwork.wordpress.com/the-in-defence-of-youth-work-letter/, accessed 28 February 2010.

Jeffs, T. and Smith, M. (1993) Getting the Job Done, Training for Youth Work – Past, Present and Future. *Youth and Policy*, 40, Spring 1993.

Jenks, C. (2005) (second edition) *Culture*, London, Routledge.

Johnson, T. (1993) Expertise and the State. in Gane, M. and Johnson, T. (eds.) *Foucault's New Domains*, London, Routledge.

Kuenstler, P. (1955) *Social Group Work in Great Britain*, London, Faber and Faber.

Lasch, C. (1991) [1979] *The Culture of Narcissism: American Life in an Age of Diminishing Expectations*, New York, W.W. Norton and Company.

Leighton, J.P. (1972) *The Principles and Practice of Youth and Community Work*, London, Chester House Publications.

Lowe, R. (1988) *Education in the Post-War Years, A Social History*, London, Routledge.

Martin, B. (1981) *A Sociology of Contemporary Cultural Change*, Oxford, Basil Blackwell.

Matthews, J.E. (1966) *Working With Youth Groups*, London, University of London Press.

Matthewson, J.D. (1961) The Effect of National Service on the Youth of Great Britain. *Social Service Quarterly*, XXIV: 4, March–May.

Maychell, K., Pathak, S. and Cato, V. (1996) *Providing for Young People, Local Authority Youth Services in the 1990s*, Slough, NFER.

Miles-Davies, A.E. (1945) Internal Memo Written to Fleming, Pearson and Sir Robert Wood, 1 June 1945, PRO ED 124/16.

Ministry of Education (1949) *Report of the Committee on Recruitment, Training and Conditions of Service of Youth Leaders and Community Centre Wardens*, (Jackson Report) London, HMSO.

Ministry of Education (1951) *The Recruitment and Training of Youth Leaders and Community Centre Wardens*, Second Report of the National Advisory Council on the Training and Supply of Teachers, (Fletcher Report), London, HMSO.

Ministry of Education (1953) *Education in 1952*, Being the Report of the Ministry of Education and the statistics of publication for England and Wales. (Presented by the Minister of Education to Parliament by Command of Her Majesty, June 1953) (Cmd 8835).

Ministry of Education (1954) *Education in 1953*, Being the Report of the Ministry of Education and the statistics of publication for England and Wales. (Presented by the Minister of Education to Parliament by Command of Her Majesty, June 1954) (Cmd 9155).

Ministry of Education (1960) *The Youth Service in England and Wales*, Report of the Committee Appointed by the Minister of Education in November 1958, London, HMSO.

National College for the Training of Youth Leaders (1966) *Content of Course and Method of Work*, Leicester, NCTYL.

Perkin, H. (1989) *The Rise of Professional Society, England Since 1880*, London, Routledge.

Rogers, C. (1967) *On Becoming a Person*, London, Constable.

Sennett, R. (1986) *The Fall of Public Man*, London, Faber and Faber.

Tinkler, P. (2001) Youth's Opportunity? The Education Act of 1944 and Proposals For Part-Time Continuation Education, *History of Education*, 30: 1, 77–94.

Turner, V. (1997) *The Ritual Process: Structure and Anti-Structure*, New Brunswick, Aldine Transaction.

Watkins, O.C. (1971), *Professional Training for Youth Work, Educational Method at the National College for the Training of Youth Leaders, 1961–1970*, Leicester, Youth Service Information Centre.

Youth Service Inspectors Advisory Committee, (1944), Paper written by A.E. Miles-Davies summarising the Inspectors' discussion on 25 May 1944, and correspondence received in response to the Report of the McNair Committee, PRO ED 124/16.

CHAPTER 7

Crossing Borders: Reflections on Scotland's First Experimental Youth Centre

Annette Coburn and Brian McGinley

This chapter illustrates the history of The Key Youth Centre in East Kilbride and provides a longitudinal consideration of the dispositions, orientations and actions of young people and youth workers. The Key, which celebrated its 40th birthday in 2010, was when it opened, Scotland's only experimental and purpose-built local authority youth facility. The story of The Key is one of innovation and creativity that can be reflected upon and compared to present practices in ways that might inform and inspire future hopes and expectations.

The chapter presents a 'pen picture' of the chronological development of The Key Youth Centre which shows how the facility responded to changing influences in the lives of young people, including policy and practice environments and wider social developments. The chronology is organised from three different points in history, coinciding with changes in local government which brought different demands, approaches and priorities to the centre. The chapter outlines and interrogates practice to consider how The Key transcended organisational boundaries and political upheaval. The first time period starts from the opening of the centre in 1970 and runs until 1975 when regional and district councils were formed in Scotland. The second considers developments from that time until 1996 and then, with the establishment of unitary authorities, the third section takes the narrative from 1996 up to the present day, operating under the stewardship of South Lanarkshire Council.

Background and context

The publication of the Albemarle Report (Ministry of Education, 1960) provided an opportunity to develop youth work in England and Wales that heralded a period of investment in facilities, with £28 million being spent between 1960 and 1968 on 3000 building projects and youth work training (Smith and Doyle, 2002;

Ministry of Education, 1961). In Scotland the Kilbrandon Report (HMSO, 1961) which was principally concerned with children in trouble with the law, established the Children's Hearings system and paved the way for investment in the creation of 'school wings' as a base for youth work. Increased evening use of schools and community halls for youth work and investment in youth facilities, it was argued, were necessary because adolescents were restricted by law or parental control from accessing adult facilities and had substantial leisure time but few responsibilities (Hendry, 1983: 108).

The Key Youth Centre was built in East Kilbride, one of five new towns created in Scotland to help solve a post-war housing shortage. Lack of local youth facilities and other amenities in the new towns encouraged territorialism and gang violence. However the new towns offered homes, particularly for young families, which were designed to meet modern day living needs and aspirations, and were in almost every respect superior to those in the inner-city areas that most of the inhabitants came from. East Kilbride attracted young families because of its proximity to Glasgow and its ability to offer decent living accommodation, excellent shopping facilities, and social amenities. Most importantly it also offered incomers good quality, sustainable jobs due to the modern, purpose-built office and industrial accommodation that attracted major national and international companies, such as Rolls Royce, Motorola and Coca Cola, as well as Government Departments, for example the Inland Revenue, Overseas Development and National Engineering Laboratory.

The earliest days

Three agencies, the Scottish Office, the Burgh of East Kilbride and Lanark County Council collaborated to provide the capital funding to create an experimental youth centre for East Kilbride. When it opened it was considered to be ahead of its time in architectural design (Royal Commission on the Ancient and Historical Monuments of Scotland, 2010). Its location at the heart of the new town, adjacent to the Dollan Baths and the main shopping and leisure facilities, enhanced its uniqueness as a facility that aimed to model innovative practice and experimental approaches to youth work. The Key was officially opened in 1970 and it was envisaged from the start that 'the day to day running of the experimental centre was managed by a committee of young people' (RCAHMS, 2010). The experiment in self-management involved the young people in naming the facility. The winning entry was chosen because of its rationale that the facility was for the Youth of East Kilbride (YEK) which in reverse produced KEY. This was also a useful metaphor for unlocking potential and opening doors that was part of the youth work ethos. Membership was open to anyone between the ages of 15 and 21 and they were encouraged to hang around in the café area whenever the facility was open without a requirement to participate in any of the groups or activities on offer. This was similar to the Albemarle approach which stated that young people's 'freedom of choice matches their independence and their growing maturity' (Ministry of Education 1960: 10).

Maintenance, staffing and running costs for the centre were met by the local authority's Education Department. The collaboration between Burgh, County and the Scottish Office, who were all represented on the Board of Management, produced a flow of financial investment. Thus, from its inception The Key was directly linked with Scottish policy development and under regular national scrutiny. In particular this helped attract central government funding to pilot new ideas such as the Youth Enquiry Service and the Youth Action Team (YAT) Card, a forerunner of the Young Scot Card and the European Youth Card.

The Key provided youth work for young people throughout East Kilbride, which by 1960 had a population of 50,000 that has since risen to over 74,000. The two-storey centre incorporated a games hall the size of three badminton courts, four good-sized general use rooms and two small group rooms that hosted a range of activities or provided spaces for impromptu activity and group discussion. Luxurious extras included a dedicated café hub (described initially as a 'tea-bar' and later as a 'dry pub') that accommodated 140 people in seating, with an open floor space for dancing. This area hosted discos and live gigs, in addition to providing a large informal meeting space or, with some rearrangement of seating, a make-shift cinema. In the 1970s, not every household had a colour television, and on one occasion young people queued for over 200 yards outside of the centre just to watch a European football match 'in colour'. The *Youth Service Building Bulletin* issued by Ministry of Education in England in 1961 suggesting the design of the Albemarle centres, may have had some impact on the plans for The Key. However there is no record of this. The architect, Alexander Buchanan Campbell, who had worked with the more famous modernist architect Jack Coia, was also responsible for the nearby swimming pool (which became a Category A listed building in 2002).

The facility was staffed by four qualified or qualifying youth workers (in the case of two trainees in the 70s) and three caretakers/stewards, who worked on rotational 'continental shifts' and whose job description included caretaking and cleaning duties with a requirement to engage with young people during evenings. This group was complemented by a small number of part-time staff, employed a couple of hours each week, plus 25 to 30 volunteers, around 10 of whom were older club members. From the beginning The Key opened from 9 a.m. to 10 p.m. seven days a week. The nightly programme varied, focusing on sport, arts, health and music. Saturdays were reserved for private functions, providing community groups and members with a cheap venue for fund-raising or celebration events. These bookings also generated income for the Members' Fund. A nominal annual membership fee of three shillings (fifteen pence) was charged: this was equivalent to the cost of a single cinema ticket. The programme burst with activities, classes, challenges and events offering a staple diet that included peer education programmes, girls' work, work with boys, residentials, outdoor education, training, issue-based work and fund-raising.

The regional years

The Local Government (Scotland) Act 1973 created a two-tier structure of regional and district councils. This meant a new authority, the Strathclyde Regional Council, became the owner of The Key and oversight fell to their newly formed Community Education Department that integrated youth work, community development and adult education under one umbrella (HMSO, 1975). The re-organisation left the partnership and collaborative management arrangements at The Key intact, although a clearer and helpful policy direction emanated from Strathclyde's Community Education Department. Over time this included strategic documents such as *Social Strategy for the Eighties*, Member/Officer reports on working with young people, and the Working Party on Schools and Colleges as Community Resources (SRC, 1982; 1984). Within this environment The Key was able at times to use its partnership arrangements to resist bureaucratic processes that threatened to thwart innovation and risk when responding to young people's needs.

Throughout the late seventies and early eighties The Key was brought closer into Strathclyde's organisational arrangements and was used to exemplify good practice for other workers and community representatives who aspired to establish a youth centre in a different part of the region through Urban Programme funding. East Kilbride was not eligible for such funding because it did not match the criteria. This allowed The Key to continue its experimental approach as it avoided the reporting regimes imposed by the Urban Programme, and it flourished through a combination of support from local business and a reputation for innovative practice. It also established a continuous, enjoyable fund-raising culture and an extensive commitment from young people, volunteers and youth workers.

Arguably being ineligible for Urban Programme money combined with young people's autonomous spending power and a strong fund-raising ethos enabled The Key to be maintained and staffed to an appropriate level. This may have helped it to survive as a youth facility, to weather cuts in public spending and moves towards multi-use buildings. For example, the annual membership levy supplemented the local authority contribution to running costs, but a nightly fee of five pence, which was increased as and when the members' committee decided, was also charged to generate income for the Members' Fund. This was controlled by young people thus enabling them to have a significant measure of influence over programme content. For example the Members' Fund was used to subsidise trips and visits, to underwrite the refurbishment of the café and other parts of the building and to contribute to the wages of specialist part-time staff.

Local 'gangs' and 'young teams' were welcome in The Key. However, despite being located at the town centre, in what was envisioned as neutral territory, there were always problems, both then and now. It is acknowledged that young people from some areas found it difficult to travel across territorial boundaries to reach the facility. So despite an open-door policy some young people felt unable to attend. This remains problematic. The issue of territorialism is one which has plagued Scotland for many years and although there are positive benefits in the sense of belonging to a group of trusted friends, this issue can be negatively formed around larger areas or individual streets (Wallace and Coburn, 2002). Territorialism presents a challenge to youth workers in determining whether to try to bring people together or to offer programmes in different locations. Throughout the 1980s as part of a developing response to this problem, detached and outreach work and ten satellite youth clubs helped young people from different local neighbourhoods to access a minimal level of youth work, whilst also breaking down barriers and encouraging them to come to The Key.

Strathclyde Council published *Working with Young People* (SRC, 1984) which helpfully called for increased participation by young people in their communities and targeted work in rural areas, with young women and across a range of abilities. It also identified specialist areas for future development such as international work, participatory democracy, outdoor education and the arts.

This strategy could have been written with The Key in mind because its value base was grounded in the entitlement of all to participate in society and in the need to challenge discrimination and inequality. This was present within The Key in the focus on an informal education based on a critical pedagogy (Freire, 1972). These methods fostered problem posing education where loving and respectful relationships among workers and young people thrived. Those who were isolated because of ability and economic factors, or who experienced long-term unemployment were encouraged to participate in every aspect of the facility. Positive discrimination helped ensure that those most vulnerable to exclusion could choose to participate. Gender inequality was challenged around the pool table and in the DJ sub-committee that involved young men and women in running what was effectively a small business enterprise in 1975. This generated a significant income for the Members' Fund and for the young people themselves, who received payment for DJing 'gigs' and by the time of its tenth birthday celebrations The Key had generated sufficient income to establish Key TV with a video camera the size of a small house and an 8-track sound recording studio.

Encouraged by this supported and visionary policy environment, a single gender gym night was introduced in 1985 building on a long established weight training group that previously only attracted young men. Through the Members' Fund new equipment was purchased for the gym such as rowing machines, a treadmill and 'steps'. These items complemented the existing equipment to create a health and fitness club for young women as part of a dedicated nightly theme. International work also increased at this time, building on existing Town Twinning arrangements to enable young people to develop nine partnerships that supported international and cultural exchanges. Throughout this period the numbers attending The Key were routinely between 150 and 200 young people per night but by the mid-1990s, this had fallen to between 80 and100. Attendance levels and patterns changed in light of commercial developments in the town centre, notably the presence of a multi-screen cinema and ice rink, and despite having state-of-the-art computing equipment, young people were spending more time playing games at home, than coming to the centre (Hendry, Shucksmith, Love and Glendinning, 1993). Nevertheless, at the height of the recession in the 1980s, and again in the early 1990s, daytime numbers rose significantly due to high unemployment rates and the introduction of an alternative to mainstream school programmes. However, the lowering of numbers participating in evening youth work sessions, consistent with trends elsewhere (Smith, 1988) signalled a need for change.

The South Lanarkshire years to date 2010

The 1994 Local Government (Scotland) Act introduced a single tier unitary local authority which commenced on the 1 April 1996, opening an opportunity to revisit youth services across the newly created authority area. In the early days of the new council, during a public meeting, the council leader responded to calls for more things to do for young people by highlighting an extensive building and refurbishment programme for new sports and swimming facilities. It is reported that one young man at the back of the room quipped, 'Yea councillor, and is that what you do at the weekend, go for a swim?' And so the seeds were sown for an extensive review of youth services and a new envisioning of youth work policy. Drawing on experiences from The Key, contemporary internet café developments and other leisure time provision, a new network of integrated youth facilities was proposed to create informal learning hubs through which young people could participate in learning and be supported to achieve their full potential (SLC, 2008). The Key became one of ten major youth service centres operated under the auspices of the local authority in collaboration with a number of partner agencies.

Thus 40 years on, there remains a dedicated youth facility, now called Universal Connections at The Key (Universal Connections being the umbrella term used to identify the network of dedicated youth facilities). Upgraded through authority-wide investment in youth services and funded through a process of top-slicing departmental budgets to support corporate developments, the facility now incorporates an alternative school in two of the four GP rooms. The facility is staffed by eight full-time youth workers who combine youth work with general cleaning or caretaking duties. There are no caretakers so immediate requirements and opening times are 'covered' by full-time youth workers while routine cleaning is undertaken by two cleaners, employed for three mornings each week. Youth workers are qualified to varying levels and each year a small number are supported to participate in Continuing Professional Development to improve practice by ensuring staff are appropriately qualified. There are now fewer adult volunteers and these tend to be linked to specific groups such as disability sports or the youth award schemes. However young people are still encouraged to volunteer their services to share talents, develop self and help others.

Nowadays the building remains as a dedicated generic youth facility with 'drop-in' capacity on three nights plus a Saturday daytime programme. It also targets excluded young people and encourages those seeking to break away from 'gangs' by offering alternative activities that appear to be grounded in a similar value base of entitlement, love and respect between diverse groupings of facility users. The young people, both then and now, praise the centre and youth workers, citing experiences of identity formation and personal transformation and their appreciation at having a safe place to hang around. Among workers there is consensus regarding the value of the voluntary participation of young people in informal educational youth work and positive relationships that enable impromptu group sessions or conversation based learning. Yet there are also examples of targeted work that has responded to current needs and policy agendas, for example, young carers or young people in the MC2 grouping. MC2, 'More Choices, More Chances', is the current political response in Scotland to young people who are not in education, employment or training, or are at risk of becoming so labelled (Scottish Government, 2006).

Lessons learned

We now consider the Members' Committee as an example of practice which illuminates the aspiration of youth participation in local decision-making. In the 1970s and 1980s it was integral to the running of the centre. This grouping and its various sub-committees organised the programme and generated sufficient income to employ part-time staff, refurbish the café and other areas, and to purchase sound engineering, computing and other equipment or materials to support learning. Fund-raising activity enabled young people to bond more closely by participating in enjoyable events such as street tiddly-winks, dry land windsurfing and celebrity 'kidnap'. The Members' Committee synthesised decision-making with support and confidence building by forming a diverse social group that mobilised action with and for other young people. One youth worker supported the Members' Committee taking time to get to know the members and facilitating their learning about such things as budgeting or staff selection. However the worker had no voting rights or power of veto, beyond ensuring that decisions were lawful and unlikely to cause offence. This was in keeping with the policies of the day that suggested, 'young people themselves should have the power to cause change and actively work towards the services they desire or need' (SRC, 1984: 16). By 1989 the Members' Committee had merged with the management committee and young people were now fully-fledged office bearers. Power was inclined towards young people as evidenced in their management of funds, selection of staff and an empowering narrative within authority-wide youth strategies.

By 2000 a Youth Council had become the authority-wide response to facilitating the articulation of youth voice. One youth worker was designated as supporting Youth Council members for each area within a structure that encouraged participation and active citizenship. A facility 'users' group' also supported the young people's agency, taking decisions and becoming involved in other aspects of running the facility. The language of 'facility user' was a change that it could be argued, repositioned young people as a users of services provided for them by others, as distinct from their working in collaboration with other young people and youth workers. By 2007 young people were no longer involved in staff selection, fund-raising activity was limited or project-specific, and their use of discretionary decision-making powers on spending had been curtailed. The two structures for participation in decision-making then and now, are illustrated in the table overleaf.

Both the Members' Committee and Youth Council have fulfilled a function in terms of personal benefits to participants and in their understanding of power within the contexts of area-wide and facility decision-making. However consideration of whose interests were served by decisions taken suggested that the level of change that either grouping was able to influence was limited. To an extent this was consistent with literature that suggested participation structures were beneficial but did not facilitate changes in how society viewed or included young people in democratic processes (McCulloch, 2007). Within youth policy development there was increased involvement of some young people in decision-making and in negotiating the content and action around policy implementation, yet arguably these were, 'ticking the boxes and missing the point' (Batsleer, 2008: 141).

This is most obvious in the Youth Council, which at the time of writing, is engaged in many activities that tick boxes in terms of personal development, confidence building and increasing skill level that are in keeping with trends in new

The two structures for participation

Members Committee (1970–1996)	Youth Council (1997–Present)
• Members' committee work was focused on the facility and its immediate environs. • Young people routinely raised funds, generated income and determined spending on a variety of projects and equipment. • Young people shared power with workers in selection of part-time staff. • Young people sometimes relied on youth workers for support and for funding information. • The members committee met and took decisions with no requirement to have a support worker present.	• Youth councillors influenced policy development across all community planning agendas (education, health, housing, policing) and wider geographical areas. • Youth councillors had limited discretionary spending power. • The young people were often guided by youth workers and not routinely involved in staff selection. • Young people often relied on workers for support and funding. • A worker was always present in youth council meetings and when decisions were taken.

public management (McLaughlin, Osborne and Ferlie, 2002). The young people are also engaged in decision-making. However, the Youth Council is influenced by non-youth work adults in other parts of the local authority and policy sphere who direct the kind of decisions they are able to take. At a national and authority level the language of empowerment has almost disappeared from policy: the youth councillors who have no formal powers seek, through pre-determined and often adult led structures, to influence those who have power (Youth Council, 2009). The language is honest in not claiming influence where there is none. Young people do influence policy development via consultations that are youth friendly and through the Corporate Connections Board, but topics appear to be generated within a community planning framework rather than starting with young people's agendas (Youth Council, 2009). The long term significance, benefit and impact of this type of approach has been identified as limited due to the involvement of 'insider' youth and adults, reduced engagement in real decision-making, and difficulties in providing evidence of impact on young people's lives beyond the small group of those directly involved (McGinley and Grieve, 2010).

The Members' Committee, as operated in past times, was less obviously adult controlled because they often met on their own and had some freedom, within legal parameters, to explore and develop possibilities for action that included taking responsibility for programmes and purchasing equipment. It also operated within constraints that required specific actions in relation to policy imperatives where decisions to comply or not, brought consequences in terms of funding. The current users' group does work collectively for change within the facility, so there is some evidence of progress, despite the use of less emphatic language of empowerment.

There appears to have been a shift in the worker's role from floating ideas to selling them, from making suggestions to directing activity. This shift is most often noted in terms of meeting the demands of funding requirements and the pressure to measure outcomes reflecting the changing perspectives of society towards young people in seeking to control them (Mizen, 2004; Smart, 2007).

This illustration also suggests the simulated nature of youth participation (McCulloch, 2007) and calls into question the existing distribution of power. For example in the 2000s the authenticity of the process, in terms of young people's capacity to assert power, was questioned when staff absence meant a meeting was cancelled. Alternatively in the 1970s and 1980s, the Members' Committee was encouraged to meet and take decisions or grapple with ideas whether a worker was present or not. This seems to reflect shifting societal perspectives but it appears that young people and youth workers in each time frame were constrained by boundaries that restricted their capacity to renegotiate power hierarchies. These boundaries seem more obvious now than before because increased funding and impact-driven youth work across the UK means that staff are less inclined to take risks preferring the safety of pre-established outcomes (Morgan, 2009).

Arguably in both the 1970s and since 2000, opportunities to engage in exploration of the relationship between the personal and the political had begun but were not sufficiently developed to facilitate a challenge to hierarchical relations and domination. Nevertheless, young people expressed feelings of collective agency and new possibilities were explored. In the 1970s there was a sense of freedom, and power sharing operated in ways that enabled young people at times to 'have the power to cause change' (SRC, 1984: 16). This appears to have been distilled over time into a mechanism for a more simulated form of participation and consultation but at a local level, there is no doubting the commitment and intentions of workers who demonstrate good progress in the level of collaboration between agencies, departments and local youth councils. In spite of the limitations identified by McGinley and Grieve (2010) this revised structure appears to have improved since the 1970s, in one particular dimension: namely that the professional and territorial boundaries are now crossed to enable young people to influence area and authority wide policies. In contrast the Members' Committee had focused exclusively on the youth work setting itself.

Conclusion

This chapter has reflected on young people and youth workers' experiences of The Key spanning a 40 year period. The findings are in keeping with those of Robertson (2005) who articulated what a good youth club can be. The Key offered, and continues to offer, an open setting within which young people benefit from high quality associational peer relationships, informal and respectful adult relationships, and opportunities to experience situations and events that they could not achieve on their own. Robertson (2005) also highlights the importance of working over the long-term and having fun. There is also evidence of commonality in the formation of trusting relationships and, at times, an exercising of power and autonomy by young people. In this way The Key (and arguably UC at The Key) may be positioned as a site of history making that extends possibilities for collaborative informal learning between young people and youth workers as affirmed by Tett (2010) where young people can exercise their rights and make informed choices. Youth work may be proposed as a 'dissenting vocation' where workers are on the side of young people in the same way that adult education has at time operated, 'against the ideological and economic forces that seek to dominate, oppress and exploit' (Martin, 2001 quoted in Tett, 2010: 107). Reflecting on past and present histories of The Key we can see it has been agile at keeping officialdom at arm's length while also engaging directly with funding and policy initiatives that benefit young people. In essence this facility appears to have sustained an experimental base that transcends policy and governance mechanisms by 'sticking to the knitting' (Young, 1998) and working across disciplinary and political boundaries. Quality youth work experiences have inspired young people (then and now) to be hopeful about their futures. In part, this may be attributed to their involvement in useful learning within the Experimental Key Youth Centre.

40 years of The Key

Date	Key Event
10 Oct 1970	Key Youth Centre Official Opening Ceremony performed by Provost Bill Niven.
1974	Radio 1, Youth Club Call, Alan 'fluff' Freeman calls in for a live Broadcast.
1975	First Key drama group performance of *The Jungle Book*, at the neighbouring Dollan Baths; Trip to see new band, Queen, at Apollo Theatre.
1976	Roller Skating is offered as a new activity.
1980	A week of 10th Birthday celebrations include a visit by Jock Stein, an It's a Knockout event involving past and present staff and members, Arts and Sports Showcase events, the birth of Key TV using state of the art video (camera the size of a small house!) and installation of 8 Track recording studio.
1981	Established twinning link with BallerupUngdomskolle, Denmark.
1982	Youth training arrives with the first of many programmes targeting long term unemployed.
1983	Innovative collaboration established with High St Building Society to open an outreach depositing service to encourage young people to get into the habit of saving.
1985	UN International Youth Year: Drama group collaboration with Channel 4 to produce EKOK for broadcast on National TV Network; Youth Action Team (YAT) discount card as a pilot for the emerging YoungScot card. YAT Card supporters include Olympic runner

	Sandra Whitacker, Actress Dee Hepburn and Footballer Ali McCoist; First Youth Exchange to Erlangen.
1986	Launch of International Contacts Group to oversee extensive youth exchange programme involving cultural exchanges with over 7 countries.
1988	Launch of Rockschool Project: collaboration of young musicians and people in the local music scene to foster learning about the music industry and promote live gigs and other music related activity and recording opportunities.
1988	Key workers are part of national writing team for modules in Young Enterprise, to be rolled out in Secondary Schools in Scotland.
1990	Satellite Juke Box: the Key was the only Live Scottish venue chosen by MTV highlights of this 24 hour event included appearances by Lorraine Kelly, Runrig, Hugh Red and the Velvet Underpants and legendary locals, Jacobilly Bush Box.
1991	Key workers are part of a module writing and delivery team to develop Scotvec 71480: An Introduction to Youth Work. This is a forerunner in development of various SQA level qualifications for youth work in Scotland.
1994	Youth Clubs UK Award Ceremony in London.
1996	'Scenes from the heart of a crab-apple' performance using drama and photographic installation at EK Arts Centre as part of HEBS /Fastforward national programme on Young people and Mental Health.
1997	The Key closes for refurbishment in May.
1998	Key refurbished and re-named as Universal Connections at the Key.
1999	'Chumble' environmental junk band formed, delivering workshop to community groups throughout South Lanarkshire; EK Youth Disability Sports group formed.
2000	Millennium celebration event hosted by South Lanarkshire Youth Council.
2001	Teenage Health Information Service Launched; Young people research and produce film called 'BLAME' on the effects of crime, funded by Prudential.
2003	Young people work with developers to create purpose built wheeled and extreme sports skate-park.
2004	Roll out of Youth Achievement Awards to accredit young people's learning. YELL celebration of the arts.
2005	Drama group Vertigo Theatre commissioned to research, write and perform ground breaking play to commemorate 60 years of the holocaust themed 'Survivors Liberation and Rebuilding Lives'.
2006	East Kilbride young people host Young Scot Health Event. Launch of INFEST music festivals. Youth workers and young people interviewed by BBC Radio Scotland's programme Action Scotland – underage drinking.
2007	Successful Cash Back for Communities bid to replace Games Hall floor and refurbish changing facilities with Disability Sports Partners. Young people raise funds for OXFAM through OXJAM music events.
2008	Work together with 'Problem Solving Policing' group to develop work and to further refurbish basement, including dedicated group work room, art room and music rehearsal space.
2009	Young people created own virtual island called Dharma through teen second life and Core Connex; Perpetual sunlight experienced on cultural exchange to Finland.
2010	Development of 'Green Room' recording studio. Two young people from East Kilbride win SOLVE Volunteer of the Year Awards and Runner up 16+ Participate in National Research Project with Learning & Teaching Scotland called 'Hypothetically Speaking'.

References

Batsleer, J. (2008) *Informal Learning in Youth Work*, London, Sage.

Freire, P. (1972) *Pedagogy of the Oppressed*, London, Penguin.

Hendry, L.B. (1983) *Growing Up and Going Out*, Aberdeen, Aberdeen University Press.

Hendry, L., Shucksmith, J., Love, J.G. and Glendinning, A. (1993) *Young People's Leisure and Lifestyles*, London, Routledge.

HMSO (1975) *Adult Education: The Challenge of Change*, (The Alexander Report) Edinburgh, HMSO.

HMSO (1961) *The* Kilbrandon Report: *Children and Young Persons Scotland*, Edinburgh, HMSO.

Jeffs, T. and Smith, M.K. (2006) Where is *Youth Matters* Taking Us? *Youth and Policy* 91, 23–40.

McCulloch, K. (2007) Democratic Participation or Surveillance? Structures and Practices for Young People's Decision-Making. *Scottish Youth Issues Journal* 9, 9–22.

McGinley, B. and Grieve, A. (2010) Maintaining the Status Quo? in B. Percy-Smith and N. Thomas (eds.) *A Handbook of Children and Young People's Participation*, London, Routledge.

McLaughlin, K., Osborne, S.P. and Ferlie, E. (2002) *New Public Management: Current Trends and Future Prospects*, London, Routledge.

Ministry of Education (1960) *The Youth Service in England and Wales* (The Albemarle Report) http://www.infed.org/archives/albemarle . . . report/index.htm.

Ministry of Education (1961) *Youth Service Building: General Mixed Clubs* (Bulletin 20) London, Ministry of Education.

Mizen, P. (2004) *The Changing State of Youth*, Basingstoke, Palgrave.

Morgan, T. (2009) Measuring Outcomes in Youth Work in Northern Ireland. *Youth and Policy*, 103, 49–64.

Robertson, S. (2005) *Youth Clubs: Association, Participation, Friendship and Fun*, Lyme Regis, Russell House.

Royal Commission on the Ancient and Historical Monuments of Scotland (2010). *East Kilbride, Brouster Hill, The Key Experimental Youth Centre* (Retrieved 10/10/10) http://canmore.rcahms.gov.uk/en/site/166203/details/east + kilbride + brouster + hill + the + key + experimental + youth + centre/

Scottish Government (2006) *More Choices, More Chances: A Strategy to Reduce the Proportion of Young People not in Education, Employment or Training in Scotland*, available @ http://www.scotland.gov.uk/Publications/2006/06/13100205/0

SLC (2008) *Universal Connections: Our Journey to Excellence: Celebration Report*, Hamilton, South Lanarkshire Council.

Smart, S. (2007) Informal Education, (In)Formal Control? What is Voluntary Youth Work to Make of Self-Assessment. *Youth and Policy* 95, 73–82.

Smith, M.K. and Doyle M.E. (2002) The Albemarle Report and the Development of Youth Work in England and Wales, *The Encyclopaedia of Informal Education*, http://www.infed.org/youthwork/albemarle . . . report.htm (10/10/10).

Smith, M. (1988) *Developing Youth Work; Informal Education, Mutual Aid and Popular Practice*, Milton Keynes, Open University Press.

SRC (1984) *Working with Young People*, Glasgow, Strathclyde Regional Council.

SRC (1982) *Report of the Working Party on Schools and Colleges as Community Resources*, Glasgow, Strathclyde Regional Council.

Tett, L. (2010) *Community Education, Learning and Development* (3rd Edition) Edinburgh, Dunedin.

Wallace, D. and Coburn, A. (2002) Space, The Final Frontier: An Exploration of Territoriality and Young People. *Scottish Youth Issues Journal*, 73–92.

Young, K. (1998) Sticking to the Knitting. *Youth and Policy* 60, 84–9.

Youth Council (2009) Home Page retrieved at www.youthcouncil.lanlinks.org (12/2/10).

CHAPTER 8

The Kingston Youth Service: Space, Place and the Albemarle Legacy

Jon Ord

Altogether, approximately 3,000 new youth club buildings were completed during the 1960s in England and Wales following publication of the Albemarle report (Davies, 1999; Robertson, 2005). This chapter focuses upon the impact of that building programme upon one locality. It is based on discussions undertaken during 2008 in the outer London Borough of Kingston-upon-Thames, where the author was a local authority youth worker from 1994 to 2003. A number of youth workers were interviewed regarding Kingston's 'Albemarle legacy' and these, as well as my own reflections, provide the basis for the following narrative. This 'story' does not claim to be definitive and other perspectives exist, but it draws on the experiences of people who were, and in some cases remain, key members of staff within the Kingston Youth Service.[1] All five centres constructed in Kingston during the immediate post-Albemarle years remain operational and their history reflects the importance of 'place' and 'space' in youth work. A significant theme is one of long term under-investment in youth work staff and premises during the last half century. It should be noted that the Albemarle 'project' was about much more than the provision of new buildings. It embodied an attempt to significantly develop 'club-based' youth work. Buildings were important in this process, but so too were the relationships youth workers developed with young people.

Albemarle's building programme

Publication of the Albemarle report proved a seminal moment in the history of youth services in England and Wales; as Davies notes, 'If the youth service ever had a golden age then the 1960s were certainly it' (1999: 57). Albemarle advocated 'a generous and imaginative building programme as essential to rehabilitate the Youth Service and to equip it for the expansion that is called for' (1960: 65, para. 224). Subsequently, an unprecedented building programme was initiated, predominately funded via Ministry of Education grants. Albemarle also stressed 'the need for standards to be raised in furniture, lighting, decoration and equipment as well as in the buildings themselves' (1960: 68, para. 233). The advice was heeded and during the post-publication decade £23 million was spent on nearly 3,000 building projects (Davies, 1999: 61) The cost of the Chessington Youth Centre, built in 1960, was £13,000 (*Surbiton Borough News*, c. August 1960). This might be compared with the average cost today of £4 million for a new multi-agency youth centre funded within the Myplace scheme (HM Treasury, 2007; Big Lottery Fund, 2009).

Kingston received a grant to construct five large youth and community centres. The records of the Borough Valuer give the following completion dates for these as:

Hook Youth and Community Centre:	financial year 1965/66
Chessington Youth and Community Centre:	financial year 1965/66
Doris Venner Youth and Community Centre:	financial year 1967/68
Barnfield Youth and Community Centre:	financial year 1968/69
Searchlight Youth and Community Centre:	financial year 1969/70

Chessington actually opened officially on 26 November 1960, before the release of the Albemarle monies, having been paid for by Surbiton District Council (*Surbiton Borough News*, 30 November 1960).[2] However a new extension was subsequently added and the funding for this, along with the cost of re-furbishing the building almost certainly came from the Albemarle grant, which explains the Borough Valuer's final completion date of 1965, and Chessington being viewed as an Albemarle centre.

All five centres listed above have enjoyed considerable longevity and for over three decades they formed the backbone of the Kingston Youth Service. Indeed until the mid-1990s they were the Borough's only statutory provision, apart from a youth club operating from an old portacabin on the Kingsnympton estate. During the 1990s the portacabin was replaced by a purpose-built centre. Around the same time a small residents' association community centre at School Lane was acquired by the local authority who converted it into a youth centre. Consequently over 40 years after they were opened, the five 'Albemarle centres' continue to form the main physical resource of the Kingston Youth Service, and it is likely they will do so for the foreseeable future.

Despite differences in external appearance, all five centres have a similar layout with each containing a large sports hall, a generous communal area and two or three smaller rooms – often utilised as offices or art rooms. This pattern reflects what Robertson termed the Albemarle 'grand plan' wherein:

> The general principles of these new buildings were outlined in the Ministry Bulletin No.20 (1961) ... they were aiming for a sophisticated physical

environment to attract young people who had not used it before. They usually offered areas for physical sporting activity, quiet rooms, a dance area and craft rooms.

(2005: 31)

Few early records relating to the life of the centres survive. Their relationship with their past is tenuous and often the only 'records' are the memories of past members and leaders. Chessington is the only one to have an archive and this includes a scrapbook of press releases and old photographs which have been used to inform this chapter. These centres were extremely popular during their early years. Jane Wray, who was both a member and worker at Chessington, recalls that up to the mid-1970s all five had at least 100 teenagers in attendance on a Friday night. The Chessington Centre replaced an older club that had operated in nearby rented accommodation since 1942. By February 1965, it had enrolled over 600 members (*Surbiton Borough News*, 1965). The membership age range was 12 to 21, and the centre opened five nights a week from 6.00 until 10.15. Often as many as 250 attended during an evening. The record appears to have been 350 who crammed into the building for a live broadcast of Alan Freeman's 1960s *Radio One Show* (ibid.).[3] For many years the Chessington Centre was run by George Nightingale who oversaw a rich and varied programme. According to an article in the *Surbiton Borough News*, headlined 'Chessington Youth Club Is Really "With It"', the club offered:

chess, football, boatbuilding, music, drama, ten pin bowling, jazz, dress making, woodwork, photography and journalism . . . as well as the traditional youth club standbys – darts, snooker, table tennis, dancing, pop music and of course the telly.

(30 November 1962)

Members performed plays and pantomimes and participated in sporting events. However there was not an undue emphasis on activities and young people often simply 'hung out' at the coffee bar. For many years Chessington offered a 'girls only night', though clearly not one influenced by second wave feminism; activities included 'deportment, poise and personality courses', as well as health and beauty classes and sports such as netball (*Surbiton Borough News*, 1965). The club ran trips and outings and regular holidays to Europe. One year the members produced and edited a two hour film of their European holiday.

The popularity of Kingston's Albemarle youth centres gradually waned so that today 30 young people is considered a good turn-out for a youth club session (Hall, 2009; Wray, 2010). The age of those attending has also fallen. The clubs were originally designed for 16 to 18 year olds, it being Albemarle's intention that they mirror student unions (Robertson, 2005). Chessington's members in the 1960s

Chessington Youth Club netball team, c. 1962–3

Socialising at 'jack's bar' in Chessington Youth Club, c. 1962–3

Youth club members outside Chessington Youth Club, c. 1962–3

were aged up to 21. However, as early as 1976 a survey found the majority of active youth club members were aged 14 to 16 (Eggleston cited in Robertson, 2005: 31). This trend continued and by the mid-1990s the most popular activities run by the Kingston Youth Service were junior clubs catering for 8 to 11s, which continue to attract up to 100 participants. Currently the target age group for most of Kingston's Albemarle centres is young people in their last two years of compulsory schooling (Hall, 2009). Times are now very different, for as Jeffs and Smith suggest:

> *the irresistible rise of commercial providers, including the expansion of home entertainment and leisure centres, has left the youth work sector a bit part player within an arena where once it was a central figure.*

> (2006: 27)

Rarely now are youth clubs central and pivotal in the lives of young people, especially those in their late teens or early twenties.

The importance of 'place'

Locations that seemed appropriate for youth centres in the 1960s are unlikely to remain so over time. The experience of the Doris Venner Youth and Community

Centre illustrates this point. By the mid 1990s this centre seemed past its 'sell-by-date' after a number of youth workers had struggled during the previous decade to make a success of it (Hall, 2009). Workers now found it necessary to build relationships through detached and outreach work. An attempt was made to rebrand the centre as The Venner, as well as developing project work around issues of interest to young people such as graffiti art, but it appeared almost impossible to re-establish it as an attractive venue for young people (ibid.). One problem was that it was located in Old Malden, a 'leafy part of town' on the edge of the borough, at least a mile and a half walk from the known concentrations of young people with whom the youth workers had contact (Hall, 2009; Mafi, 2009). Consequently, many connected with Kingston Youth Service concluded that The Venner had 'had its day'. Moreover the success of a new youth club, The Fountain Youth Centre, located in New Malden, around a mile from The Venner, partially confirmed this view. The Fountain Centre grew out of a detached project run by Majid Mafi, who argued that young people needed a new place to meet (Hall, 2009; Mafi, 2009). Kingston Youth Service responded to this 'expression of need' and secured funding from the council's Neighbourhood Committee for the transformation of an old public toilet into a youth centre. This venture successfully attracted over 40 young people to a venue that could at best accommodate 20. Soon an awning had to be constructed to provide shelter for those unable to get inside. The location of The Fountain Centre at the end of a bustling high street, and nearer to where the young people lived, was clearly a factor in its success.

'The Venner' (previously Doris Venner Youth and Community Centre)

The Fountain Youth Centre

The other Albemarle centres are not without their problems in terms of location. Barnfield Youth and Community Centre, also located in what has become an affluent part of the Borough with a large horse-riding stable adjacent to it, is not in the best of places. Perhaps even more problematic is the location of The Searchlight Youth and Community Centre, which although not too far from Kingston's largest social housing estate, is set next to a park and allotments and is accessed via an off-putting dark and narrow passageway.

Refurbishment and investment

According to Robertson (2005) there was a flaw at the heart of the Albemarle building programme, namely the lack of attention paid to their upkeep and the absence of continuing investment to ensure centres were built to serve new and emerging communities. Albemarle assumed that membership fees would provide the necessary income to cover maintenance costs (1960: 68, para. 233). The absence of sufficient revenue has been a thorn in the side of every youth and community centre manager in Kingston, and doubtless elsewhere. The legacy of Albemarle is, at least in part, one of under-investment and a lack of commitment from both local and central government to the youth centres created during a period of rapid growth.

The case of The Hook Youth and Community Centre provided convincing evidence for this argument. Situated in the south of the Borough, approximately two miles from The Chessington Youth Centre it, like the others, was initially extremely popular but attendance and usage waned to such an extent that by the late 1990s its viability was questioned, less because it was inappropriately located like The Venner, but because what it had to offer failed to engage young people (Hall, 2009). However this situation has been transformed. In 2006 The Hook received a £280,000 refurbishment budget from the local authority. Consequently a tired and shabby building was turned into a modern vibrant 'space' with additional 'small group' rooms and an IT suite. Rebranded as 'Devon Way' (named after the road that leads to it) it has experienced a renaissance in terms of usage (ibid.).

Interestingly the funding of the refurbishment of The Hook Youth and Community Centre did not come from the Youth Service – it was from the 'Services for Older People' budget. The centre must now equally meet the needs of both older and younger people. There have been some unforeseen benefits accruing from this additional funding source and the need to include services and activities for older people. It successfully brought together and encouraged inter-genera-tional work. The two segments of the community who were previously, at times, antagonistic towards each other now share the building and engage in dialogue both informally and in more formal 'inter-generational' gatherings such as lunches during school-holidays. At these events, older members of the community have

Intergenerational Day at 'Devon Way' (Hook Youth and Community Centre)

even been known to admit to 'getting up to no good when they were young'. Some now see even 'hoodies' in a new light.

What the experience of the Kingston Youth Service shows is that any judgement about the future of the Albemarle centres must, at least in part, be made with reference to possibilities of reinvestment and refurbishment. The refurbishment of The Hook Youth and Community Centre shows there are tangible benefits to be gained from a commitment to revive these 'tired' old centres. Young people can be persuaded to return and centre-based youth work within them can be re-energised. Indeed, the earlier absence of refurbishment in Kingston's Albemarle centres was stark; they have had next to no capital injection or investment in their lifetime. There were some limited exceptions. For instance the Chessington Centre received £2,500 from Chessington World of Adventures in 1993 to construct a new coffee bar. This helped to create a contemporary 'feel' to an outdated building but failed to make a sustained difference to the numbers attending the centre (Hall, 2009). A second example of investment relates to Barnfield Youth and Community Centre where following work undertaken in the late 1990s by a senior youth worker, a charitable arm was established which raised sufficient funding to convert part of it into a music studio, reinvigorating the centre (Smyth, 2009).

More than a building

These reflections on the history of Kingston's Albemarle centres also tell us about the importance of the 'space' created within the buildings. For example a flaw often cited with regards The Venner is its layout (Hall, 2009; Mafi, 2009). Here the communal area, unlike those in the other centres, approximates to an open hallway with glass doors at either end. Although comfortable chairs are situated in this 'room' it is unsuitable as a space for workers to sit down with young people and engage in conversation for it serves as a thoroughfare leading to the sports hall and small rooms. Therefore it best approximates to a large lobby area via which young people enter and exit the building (Mafi, 2009).

The success of The Fountain Youth Club offers a contrasting example of space. There is no sports hall or large communal room both of which characterised the five Albemarle centres. Instead here was a small 'intimate space' (Hall, 2009). Interestingly The Fountain Centre, despite its geographical proximity to The Venner, in terms of its place and space is evidently 'miles apart'. Not only is it a small intimate space but it is located at the end of the bustling high street, giving it a very different sense of place. Unfortunately these two important, related but distinct aspects of youth work and youth clubs are not always fully appreciated by those responsible for either local or national youth policy (Robertson, 2000; Barton and Barton, 2007). Certainly the success of The Fountain Youth Club is a sharp reminder of the need to pay attention to such details.

Similarly the transformation of The Hook Centre led to it acquiring a very different persona (McCabe, 2009; Hall, 2009). Not only has the building been smartened-up and brought up-to-date as a result of the general refurbishment, but the feeling of space is now different following the creation of additional small group rooms. Smith (1994) and Barton and Barton (2007) remind us that 'place' is often much more than a geographical location. For 'to talk of place is to refer to understandings and feelings – it is not simply a matter of the area within lines drawn on a map' (Smith, 1994: 10). The involvement of young people in the creation of The Fountain Youth Club and the renovation of The Hook Youth and Community Centre enabled the creation of a 'place' where they enjoy a sense of belonging.

Longevity: 'income generation' and 'community use'

Given the pace of change during the last half century it is perhaps surprising that Kingston's Albemarle centres have remained largely intact. An important but perhaps unacknowledged factor in this longevity occurred in the 1980s with the changes initiated to public service management during the Thatcher era. In Kingston, local Conservative politicians decided that the five centres should become 'income generators' and 'pay their way'. As a result each was given an income target. This proved a double edged sword. First it cut down the availability of the centres for youth work, in many cases to two evenings a week. The other evenings and the weekends were taken up by lettings to community groups, which numerically expanded the centres' clientele and broadened the spectrum of community usage. Different groups from 'play groups' to sports clubs and '50-plus bingo clubs' took place, ensuring the centres became income generators and therefore less justifiable for closure. The example of The Venner bears this out. Regarded as a failing 'youth' centre by local authority managers, it was identified for closure in 1995, but local politicians refused to endorse this decision as they feared a backlash from the local community. The success of subsequent income generation programmes validated this decision.

This new pattern of financial management for the Albemarle centres came alongside another key change in the running of the clubs. Initially their governance was in the main by a management committee comprising local residents, parents and representatives from centre user groups, councillors, local authority officers, youth workers and other interested parties. Decisions were made locally and the committee held the budgets for the centres, with any income generated by the centre spent according to the discretion of the committee. As a result management of the club was at least partially removed from local authority control; indeed the full-time worker initially submitted their annual report to the management committee. Over the years there has occurred a gradual diminution of the committee's role. By the late 1980s and early 1990s budgetary control had been taken away from them and their position was reduced to an advisory one, although they were still expected to raise funds for the club. This new situation gave the committee considerably less power but it did ensure a conduit for communication between the local authority managers and both the centres' users and the local community, who could, to an extent, via the committee influence the running of the centre. Management committees have now disappeared altogether, being gradually disbanded as it became increasingly difficult to get people to sit on a body lacking real power and purpose. The Searchlight Centre was the last to retain its committee which disbanded in 2004.

The importance of relationships

A cautionary note regarding an exclusive focus on buildings is needed here, and a recognition of the importance of relationships within youth work practice. The success of any centre is largely dependent upon the quality of the youth worker and part-time staff working there. The success of Chessington Youth and Community Centre was in no small part due to the longevity and the approach of its leader, George Nightingale (Hall, 2009; Wray, 2010). Describing the facilities on offer at the club Nightingale, in an article in the local paper, explained the success of the club: 'The secret? I don't talk down to the members – but along with them'. Clearly many parallels exist between the approach taken by Nightingale during Chessington's early years, the now accepted practices of 'mutuality', and the contemporary emphasis upon the importance of respect (Jeffs and Smith, 2005; Richardson and Wolfe, 2001; NYA, 2001). Nightingale was the full-time worker at Chessington for the first 20 years and before that had been a part-time leader for six years. Jane Wray who knew Nightingale for many years, both as a member of his club and as a part-time colleague, describes him as:

> A very kind man, who the kids really respected. You could talk to him about anything and you always felt listened to. He always encouraged you to try new things and to make decisions at the club, setting up members committees to support this. He also encouraged young people to become volunteers and part-time youth workers, and that is how I got into youth work.
>
> (Wray, 2010)

Jean Turnball demonstrated a similar commitment to youth work at The Searchlight Centre. In post for over 10 years from the early 1970s she built a thriving club founded on the relationships she had with young people (Hall, 2009). Other successful periods in the modern era (judged in terms of the numbers attending the club, levels of participation and number of senior members taking responsibility for aspects of the club) were the 11 years starting in 1987 when Gillian Hall was senior worker at Chessington; and the seven years from 1995 when Fran Smyth ran Barnfield. Longevity and consistency do not guarantee successful youth work but the experience at the Albemarle centres in Kingston suggests it is a prerequisite.

The experience of Kingston Youth Service indicates that the most successful centres are those where workers are committed to establishing 'a club' environment as opposed to 'drop-in' centres. This notion of a 'warm safe space' (Robertson, 2000) at the heart of the community which develops a sense of ownership, and has young people's participation in the decision-making embedded in its practices harks back to the ethos of Albemarle and beyond. Albemarle was never just about buildings and facilities but what the report explicitly referred to as the establishment of 'a club', through membership of which, according to the philosophy of Albemarle, young people's needs might begin to be met:

> . . . *club life provides challenges of all sorts to the young, who in meeting them satisfy the sense of achievement for which all hunger and which so many have failed to find in school or work.*
>
> (1960: 61)

What happened in the Kingston centres shows that establishing 'a club' is no easy task. It requires a great deal of commitment on the part of workers, a desire to be with young people in their communities and to engage with their lives. The task of establishing boundaries whilst maintaining respect for young people and facilitating ownership is challenging. Club life, which is difficult and time-consuming to establish, can dissipate very quickly. In some cases it disappears overnight when a key worker leaves. When youth workers moved on, or were promoted at The Searchlight in the 1980s, Chessington in 1998 and Barnfield in 2002, the speed at which their work disintegrated was dramatic.

Conclusion

It is possible that some Albemarle centres may have had their day in terms of youth work due to their locality or, as in the case of The Venner, their flawed design. There may be in some cases a need for smaller more intimate spaces such as The Fountain Centre to replace them. One should not overlook the example of The Hook Centre which demonstrates the potential for revitalising apparently tired old buildings but funding for such extensive refurbishment, is rarely available.

Kingston's Albemarle legacy, like that of perhaps many other authorities, was that it provided a foundation for their youth service (Davies, 1999; Robertson,

2005). Indeed the 'big' five centres; Barnfield, Chessington, Hook, Searchlight, and The Venner have given the service a foothold in the community which has ensured its survival in periods when other public services have encountered severe financial pressure. However, one of the main problems with large centres is that the resources become tied-up with the buildings. At times, their existence has hampered development by tying limited funding to the servicing of those centres. A large percentage of youth service budgets can be consumed by revenue and maintenance costs, often to the detriment of equipment and activities. For much of the late 1980s and 90s within Kingston there was insufficient money for activities, and consequently every penny spent on an activity had an income target attached to it. Another implication of expenditure being tied to centres was that Kingston Youth Service had no designated street-based or detached work until 2002. Indeed it was only the less than favourable Ofsted report of that year that gave the required political impetus needed for the creation of a 'street work team'.

Overall the history of Albemarle centres has been one of under investment which has mired their ability to meet the needs of young people. There is still a question as to what the next step should be for them. Should we be investing in them in order to bring them up-to-date and more viable for the twenty-first century, or say goodbye, and be prepared to make better use of the resources tied up in bricks and mortar. Yet as the outreach workers of Kingston maintain, when they meet young people on the streets, one of the first things they say is that they 'want somewhere to meet'.

Notes

1   I would like to thank the following people who have provided essential information for this research:

Hall, G. (2009) Gillian Hall who started as a part-time youth worker in the 1970s with Kingston Youth Service and subsequently worked at every level of the service becoming principal youth officer in 2001.

Mafi, M. (2009) Majid Mafi has worked with Kingston Youth Service for over 10 years, initially as a detached youth worker. He successfully established and still runs the Fountain Youth Project.

McCabe, K. (2009) Kerry McCabe runs Devon Way (previously known as Hook Youth and Community Centre) and has worked at Kingston for approximately 8 years.

Smyth, F. (2009) Fran Smyth ran Barnfield Youth and Community Centre for approximately five years until 2002.

Wray, J. (2010) Jane Wray who was a member of Chessington youth club in the 1960s. She has worked as a part-time youth worker for over 30 years at Chessington Youth and Community centre and is still involved with Chessington 'kids club'.

2   In 1965 Surbiton District Council, originally part of Surrey county council, became part of the Royal Borough of Kingston-upon-Thames, one of the new 32 London boroughs which made up Greater London.

3   Alan Freeman (of 'pop pickers' fame) regularly recorded his 'Radio One Show' at a youth club around the country. This provides a unique insight into the important place youth clubs had in popular culture in the 1960s.

References

Barton, A. and Barton, S. (2007) Location, Location, Location: the Challenges of Space and Place in Youth Work Policy. *Youth and Policy* 96, 41–9.

Big Lottery (2009) *My Place Funding* http://www.biglotteryfund.org.uk/prog_myplace.htm

Davies, B. (1999) *From Voluntaryism to Welfare State: A history of the Youth Service in England Volume 1, 1939–1979*, Leicester, Youth Work Press.

DfES (2002) *Transforming Youth Work; Resourcing Excellent Youth Services*, Nottingham, DfES.

HM Treasury (2007) *Aiming High For Young People: A Ten Year Strategy For Positive Activities*, London, HM Treasury/Department for Children, Schools and Families.

Jeffs, T. and Smith, M. (2005) *Informal Education: Conversation Democracy and Learning*, Derby, Education Now.

Jeffs, T. and Smith, M. (2006) Where is Youth Matters taking us? *Youth and Policy* 91, 23–39.

Ministry of Education (1960) *The Youth Service in England and Wales: Report of the Committee Appointed by the Minister of Education in November 1958* (The Albemarle Report) (Cmnd. 929) London, HMSO.

Ministry of Education (1961) *Youth Service Buildings: General Mixed Clubs* (Bulletin No. 20) London, Ministry of Education.

Ord, J, (2007) *Youth Work Process, Product and Practice: Creating An Authentic Curriculum in Work With Young People*, Lyme Regis, Russell House Publishing.

Richardson, L.D. and Wolfe, M. (2001) *Principles and Practice of Informal Education*, London, Routledge Falmer.

Robertson, S. (2000) A Warm, Safe, Place: An Argument For Youth Clubs. *Youth and Policy*, 70, 71–7.

Robertson, S. (2005) *Youth Clubs: Association, Participation Friendship and Fun*, Lyme Regis, Russell House Publishing.

Smith, M.K. (1994) *Local Education: Community, Conversation, Praxis*, Buckingham, Open University Press.

Surbiton Borough News, Newspaper as cited.

CHAPTER 9

Lessons from the USA National Youthworker Education Project

Sheila Oehrlein

The National Youthworker Education Project (NYEP) in the USA began in 1975 and concluded in 1980. It grew out of work being done under the leadership of Gisela Konopka at the University of Minnesota's Center for Youth Development Research and was funded by the Lilly Endowment, an Indianapolis based philanthropic organisation. The NYEP developed from Konopka's 1973 study of adolescent girls usually referred to as *Project Girl*. The intensive ten day training programme was designed to impact an individual youth worker's practice as well as an organisation's capacity to serve a diverse group of participants. Over the five year period during which it ran, nearly 600 individual youth workers from all parts of the United States participated in the project. By all accounts, the NYEP was a success but the training programme closed once the funding for the project ended.

Currently individuals from youth serving bodies and universities from across the country are engaged in conversations about professionalising youth work. These conversations invariably include deliberation regarding the form a national youth worker certification system might take. Therefore it is perhaps worthwhile to ask, can the lessons be learnt from the NYEP that might help guide the work currently being done to improve youth work practice and build youth worker expertise? This chapter examines the origins, structure and impact of the NYEP and identifies key lessons that might be gleaned from its implementation more than 30 years ago.

Gisela Konopka

It is nearly impossible to separate the NYEP from its founder, Gisela Konopka. Her passion for justice and enthusiastic commitment to young people was formed through the unique circumstances and experiences that influenced her personal life and professional career. She was born Gisela Pieper in Germany in 1910, the second of three daughters. Her parents owned a small store in Berlin and raised the girls in tiny living quarters adjacent to the shop. As a teen, she became involved in a youth movement known as Wandervogel where she first met Paul Konopka, the man who would later become her husband. She was a bookish girl and attended the University of Hamburg, studying philosophy, history and education. She was concluding her graduate studies when Hitler came into power. One of the earliest pieces of legislation passed by the Nazis excluded all Jews from the Civil Service which meant they were unable to teach in any sphere, therefore as a Jew her prospects for future study and employment in any educational setting were eliminated.

The impact of her personal experiences with youth movements, both through participation in *Wandervogel* and witnessing the rise of the Nazi youth movement, was something that Konopka carried with her for the rest of her life (Andrews, 2004). She and her future husband Paul became active in the resistance movement. Both were imprisoned numerous times and eventually had to separate and escape Germany. Paul moved to France and Konopka continued her resistance work in Austria, where she was again imprisoned. Eventually she moved to France where she reconnected with Paul. In 1941 they migrated to the United States and were married shortly after arriving in New York. Within the year they moved to Pennsylvania and Konopka began her graduate studies in social group work at the University of Pittsburgh's School of Social Work. She did her internship at the Pittsburgh Child Guidance Clinic, where she later held a staff position.

Konopka was recruited to teach at the University of Minnesota's School of Social Work in 1947. During her 31 years at that university she served as a professor of Social Work, Co-ordinator of Community Programmes at the Center for Urban and Regional Affairs, Special Assistant to the Vice-President of Student Affairs, and Director of the Center for Youth Development and Research which she founded in 1970. Her influence was not limited to Minnesota, but acquired a global reach. For example her prominence in the field of social group work led to the United States State Department asking her to help in the rebuilding of Germany during the immediate post-war period. There she played a significant role in helping to run programmes to help Germans learn democratic processes through the use of social group work (Andrews, 2004).

By 1973 Konopka was well established as an international leader in the areas of social group work and adolescent development. By this point in her career, she had published hundreds of scholarly articles, several books and held many distinguished positions. The Center for Youth Development and Research was also gaining a national reputation for its contribution to research in the area of youth development. In early 1973 the Office of Child Development of the United States Department of Health Education and Welfare asked Konopka, along with other staff from the Center, to develop a statement on the requirements for healthy adolescent development. The statement at this point in time was intended to be considered as a basis for a national youth policy (Konopka, 1973).

It was also in 1973 that the Lilly Endowment in Indianapolis (Indiana) received a funding request from the Camp Fire Girls a youth organisation founded in 1910 by Luther Gulick, then a lecturer at the Springfield College founded by the American YMCA, to train secretaries and physical education instructors and his wife Charlotte Vedder Gulick (Wo-He-Lo, 1980). In 1973 it was still a girls' only organisation but within two years it became 'co-ed'. The Camp Fire Girls asked Lilly to fund a researcher to work alongside their staff because teen girls were dropping out of Camp Fire programmes and the organisation wanted the researcher to help them learn why that was happening. The Lilly Endowment felt it was likely that other girl-serving organisations were experiencing a similar trend so chose to extend the scope of the project and instead conduct a national study. Following a national search Konopka and the Center were asked to lead a national study that became *Project Girl* (Corder-Bolz and Wisely, 1981).

Project Girl

Prior to this time adolescent girls were rarely the subjects of academic study. As Konopka (1976: 3) notes in *Young Girls: A Portrait of Adolescence*, '. . . most books on adolescence consider girls not at all or only as an afterthought'. This study would be an examination of the desires, apprehensions and future goals of adolescent girls. To ensure that *Project Girl* would encapsulate the authentic voice of the adolescent girls involved in the study Konopka rejected the use of a standardised survey or questionnaire because she felt it could not accurately capture the diversity of thought of the varied participants. Instead, a variety of research methods were used. Most of the information was gathered through interviews with individual girls using open-ended questions. Other data was assembled via reviews of professional studies, group discussions and poetry and prose written by the participants that was given voluntarily to the researchers.

In order to reach a wide variety of young women the study included girls age 12–18 from Alaska, California, Georgia, Indiana, Kentucky, Massachusetts, Minnesota, Oklahoma, Oregon, Puerto Rico, and Texas. A research co-ordinator was appointed for each state and they in turn hired two interviewers and identify participants that reflected the racial or ethnic make-up of the area. Special attention was paid to ensure girls from urban, suburban, small town and rural areas were in the pool of participants, as well as representation of various socio-economic groups. Additionally one-third of the participants in each state were to be:

1. Adjudicated delinquent, institutionalised girls.
2. Girls presently affiliated with youth organisations.
3. Girls not presently affiliated with youth organisations, but not delinquent.

One thousand interviews were taped, transcribed and coded on data cards for sorting and analysis. In the end 920 of these were included in the study, some having been dropped due to faulty recording. The interviews focused on the girls' opinions on a variety of topics including: relationships with adults, family, and friends; career choices and goals; relationships to peers and loneliness; drugs, alcohol, and sexuality; school, education and work experience; values and their social and political concerns; and experiences with youth organisations. While some similarities can be identified among sub-groups of the participants the goal of *Project Girl* was not to 'present a composite picture of the American Girl' but to illustrate the 'enormous variety of all human beings' (Konopka, 1976: 7).

Findings from Project Girl

The National Adolescent Girl Conference was held in Indianapolis in September 1975. The purpose was to review the findings of *Project Girl* and make recommendations for ways to improve services provided by youth organisations serving adolescent girls. A list of conference attendees included staff from *Project Girl*, the Lilly Endowment, University of Minnesota Center for Youth Development, local youth serving organisations (including correctional facilities) as well as leaders from national organisations such as Big Sisters, International, Camp Fire Girls of America, Girls Clubs of America, Girl Scouts of America, National Federation of Settlements and Neighborhood Centers, American Red Cross, YWCA of the USA, and 4H.

According to the *Summary of Research Findings: Konopka Study of Adolescent Girls*, prepared by Susan Wisely (1975) of the Lilly Endowment: 'The predominant finding of the study is that adolescent girls desperately want an understanding, communicative relationship with an adult who respects them as individuals'. These key findings were categorised by setting in particular – family life, school and youth organisations. *Project Girl* found that the girls wanted a respectful, loving and stable family life. They were looking for balance, not wanting parents or guardians to be too authoritative or too permissive. Within schools, the study showed that girls found school to be too autocratic and rigid and felt that there was not enough respect shown to individuals and members of minority groups.

The girls' opinions on youth organisations were especially telling. While only one-third of the participants in the study were involved with a youth organisation at the time of the interview, the vast majority mention some affiliation with an organisation at some point earlier in their lives. Most girls did not perceive that there were opportunities available to them, in part because they did not feel welcomed or because the structure of the programme was too autocratic and as a result they were in conflict with adult leaders. The quality of the adult staff was a major factor in whether or not the girls remained active in a youth organisation. Of the 759 girls who had a connection to a youth organisation only 15 said they felt they could go to a youth worker with a personal problem. Many of the girls went further and stated that they believed youth workers could not be trusted (Konopka, 1976).

On the basis of these findings Konopka made several recommendations for adults in order that they might support the healthy development of young women. She called for co-operation and co-ordination across families, schools and community organisations in order to meet the girls' needs. She implored adults to learn to say yes to young people and to recognise their potential. Konopka called on youth organisations to link girls to meaningful work, provide outlets for the 'spirit of adventure' to avoid 'canned programmes' and to encourage active participation. She also identified qualities that all adults should have if they are to work with youth and urged organisational leaders to make it a priority to ensure all staff working with youth possess these qualities. According to Konopka (1976) all adults should:

- have the capacity to listen and show respect;
- accept youth as equals;
- let youth play a significant role in programming and planning;
- accept sexuality as a healthy part of a young person's total being;
- understand the impact of alcohol and other drugs.

Leaders from the national girl-serving organisations realised that they needed to make some serious changes and called upon Konopka and the Center to create a training programme based on the findings and recommendations of *Project Girl*.

The National Youthworker Education Project

The National Youthworker Education Project (NYEP) began as a two-year commitment to train the staff of youth serving organisations to better support and understand the young women participating in their programmes. The Lilly Endowment provided the funding for the $920,688 budget needed to run the project. The NYEP targeted adult participants who were:

- in a position of supervising those working with young women;
- considered by the sponsoring agency as so promising that he/she may advance to have more influence on agency programmes;

- committed to working at least two more years with young people following participation in training;
- highly motivated to work with youth;
- interested in the two week training and wanted to do the intensive work before, during and after sessions.

The NYEP had three primary goals. First participation in NYEP would help participants understand adolescents and appreciate the wide range of normal behaviours during this stage of development. Second the programme would enable adults to be creative and rethink the ways they and their organisations might meet the needs of a wide range of young people from a variety of backgrounds. And finally, the NYEP would provide participants with information about other youth-serving organisations and an opportunity to interact with staff from other organisations in order to facilitate collaboration.

The training programme was structured as a three-step process. In step one, a group of 20 participants attended an intensive, ten-day residential seminar held in Minneapolis. Participants included two representatives of each of the eight selected national youth organisations and four from the correctional facilities represented at the National Adolescent Girl Conference of 1975. Over the course of the ten-day seminar, participants engaged in learning about each other, their organisations, youthhood, cultural diversity, sexuality, special populations and their unique challenges, and action planning. At the end of the ten-day seminar, participants created an action plan. In step two participants implemented their action plans within their organisations over the course of the next several months. Step three involved a follow-up conference where participants reported the results of the implementation of their action plans.

Sample Schedule: NYEP Education Sessions (Teeter, 1981).

Day 1   **Arrival in afternoon.** Orientation to project. Introduction of participants, their organisations. Sharing of concerns.

Day 2   **Adolescenthood** – Overview of development. Capabilities of youth, youth participation and contribution. Panel of young people. Small group discussions.

Day 3   **Cultural Diversity** – Needs of special groups of young people. Bus tour of city.

Day 4   **Adolescent Sexuality** – Overview of sexual development, a look at our own concerns and apprehensions, special challenges such as teen pregnancy, VD, incest, rape. Panel of young people.

Day 5   **Special Challenge** – Youth in court system. Overview of Juvenile Justice system, community responses. Views of young people.

Day 6   **Special Challenge (cont.)** – Issues such as chemical dependency, school drop-outs, truancy. Organisational responsibilities. Field visits to agencies.

Day 7   **Working with Young People in Crises** – Some of the serious life events which confront young people. Family conflict; conflict with schools. Developmental crises. Films and discussions.

Day 8   **Action Planning** – Process and development of individual action plans.

Day 9   **Reports on Action Plans** – Next steps and preparation for follow-up sessions.

Twin Cities Youthworker Education Project

In addition to the national work being done the Center conducted a local version of the NYEP in 1977 called the Twin Cities Youthworker Education Project (TCYEP). Based on the framework of the NYEP, the TCYEP was open to all youth-serving organisations in the Minneapolis and St Paul metropolitan area, not just girl-serving organisations. Two cohort groups participated in the training. The first cohort began in January 1977 and met once a week for six weeks. Each Thursday the group would meet on the University of Minnesota's St Paul campus for a daylong workshop. The curriculum for the TCYEP was the same as the NYEP, but condensed to a shorter time frame. The schedule was again revised for the second cohort so that when they met later that year participants attended five consecutive daylong sessions. A total of 125 local youth workers participated in the TCYEP.

NYEP evaluation results

In addition to internal evaluations of the NYEP conducted by the University of Minnesota, the Lilly Endowment conducted an external evaluation of the NYEP. This evaluation was designed by Judy Corder-Bolz of the Southwest Educational Development Laboratory. Corder-Bolz interviewed key staff members of the eight national organisations as well as staff from the Lilly Endowment and the Center, surveyed participants, and reviewed programme records and earlier evaluations of the project. This evaluation looked at effects on programmes, training, collaboration, and on changes in the range of girls served by the organisations.

The evaluation showed positive effects on programming, training and collaboration. The survey of national staff showed that a majority believed that their organisation's programming had made positive changes and that their training programme had improved as a result of participation in the NYEP. An overwhelming majority of programme participants were highly satisfied with the experience and indicated in surveys that they had gone on to train others within and outside of their organisations. Creating new partnerships was seen as the most valuable result of participation in NYEP, with the emphasis on collaboration well received both locally and nationally.

While there was virtually unanimous support for reaching a more diverse group of girls the evaluation showed limited effects on the range of girls served by participant organisations. In some cases leadership was reticent to make the kinds of changes needed to be more inclusive. In other instances there was not enough buy-in across the staff to reach a tipping point that would result in a more welcoming atmosphere. And the reticence was not unique to the adults or organisations. In some communities the girls themselves resisted inclusion because the history of exclusion led to distrust. Making changes in attitudes and behaviours in this area proved to be more intensive and did not result in any 'quick wins' which may have provided an incentive for change. Corder-Bolz noted in *An Evaluation of the National Youthworker Education Project: A Summary Report*, that is was possible that these changes could still occur, but that they would take longer to accomplish.

Conclusion: lessons learned

The NYEP was designed to impact the individual youth worker's practice and an organisation's capacity to be responsive to the needs of participants and staff. As the research showed the training programme had a positive impact on participants and produced encouraging changes in organisational capacity. Internal evaluations of the NYEP identified five integral elements that contributed to the success of the programme:.

1. diverse trainees enhanced the learning experience;
2. opportunities for reflection were as important as skills training for the adult participants;
3. shorter sessions were not as effective as 7–10 day training programmes;
4. in order to sustain change in the field of youth work, youth workers need a system of support and youth work must be recognised and valued;
5. the buy-in and support of national leadership was crucial to local successes.

The NYEP was unique in that it was inextricably linked to the voices of young people. Through *Project Girl* adolescent girls were able to articulate their desire to have connections with caring adults who respected and understood them. Konopka listened intently to these voices and framed a training programme with this end in mind. While the NYEP ended 30 years ago the lessons learned and indentified still resonate. Any contemporary work to create a national youth worker certification system in the United States would certainly be well advised to look closely at the NYEP model and incorporate those elements that proved successful and avoid the short-comings.

References

Andrews, J. (2004) Gisela Konopka and Group Work. *The Encyclopedia of Informal Education*, www.infed.org/thinkers/konopka.htm.

Andrews-Schenk, J. (2005) *Rebellious Spirit: Gisela Konopka*, Edina, MN, Beaver's Pond Press.

Corder-Bolz, J. and Wisely, S. (1981) *An Evaluation of the National Youthworker Education Project: A Summary Report*, National Federation of Settlements and Neighborhood Centers records, Box 149, folder 6.

Konopka, G. (1966) *The Adolescent Girl In Conflict*, Englewood Cliffs, NJ, Prentice-Hall.

Konopka, G. (1973) Requirements for Healthy Development of Youth. *Adolescence*, VIII 31, 1–26.

Konopka, G. (1976) *Young Girls: A Portrait of Adolescence*. Englewood Cliffs, NJ, Prentice-Hall.

Morrell, N. and Oehrlein, S. (2008) *The National Youthworker Education Project* (unpublished manuscript).

National Federation of Settlements and Neighborhood Centers records, Social Welfare History Archives, University of Minnesota Libraries. *Proposal, Extension of the National Youthworker Education Project, 1978–1979*, 1977, Box 149, folder 9.

National Youthworker Education Project Records, Social Welfare History Archives, University of Minnesota Libraries, *Attendee list and training preparation note*, 1975, Box 1, folder 2.

National Youthworker Education Project Records, Social Welfare History Archives, University of Minnesota Libraries. *Summary of Research Findings: Konopka Study of Adolescent Girls*, 1975, Box 1, folder 2.

National Youthworker Education Project Records, Social Welfare History Archives, University of Minnesota Libraries, *Small Groups in NYEP*. 1976, Box 15, folder 24.

Reid, K.E. (1981) Expansion and Professionalism, 1937–1955. in K.E. Reid (ed.) *From Character Building to Social Treatment. The History of The Use of Groups in Social Work*. Westport, CT, Greenwood.

Teeter, R. (1981) *Final Report to the Lilly Endowment, National Youthworker Education Project (NYEP) 1975–1980*, National Youthworker Education Project Records, Box 2, folder 42.

Wo-He-Lo (1980) *The Camp Fire History*, Kansas City, Missouri, Camp Fire Incorporated.

Primary Sources

National Federation of Settlements and Neighborhood Centers Records, Social Welfare History Archives, University of Minnesota Libraries.

National Youthworker Education Project Records, Social Welfare History Archives, University of Minnesota Libraries.

CHAPTER 10

Rise and Fall of the National Community Development Projects 1968–1978: Lessons to Learn?

Keith Popple

Prior to 1998, when New Labour launched the New Deal for Communities[1] the National Community Development Project (1968–1978) remained the most extensive targeted form of neighbourhood intervention in the UK.

The Community Development Projects (CDPs) were aimed at addressing poverty in what conventional wisdom believed to be 'dysfunctional communities' where it was thought that 'dysfunctional families' lived. More than 100 personnel were employed in 12 key projects and they were the key actors who shaped the direction of the work, producing a range of documents and reports which were widely influential.

Most of those employed by the projects questioned and then rejected conservative and traditional explanations of poverty and inner city deprivation that ultimately blamed the poor for their situation. Instead they offered a radical critique of the way in which the lives of residents in those communities were impoverished by inequality, discrimination and broader financial forces.

This chapter examines the evolution of these experimental projects launched over 40 years ago and what they achieved and the lessons we can draw from their work.

Background

After the post-war years of economic rebuilding and significant social change, which included the establishment of the welfare state, by the late 1960s, the British economy was experienced a deepening crisis that led to mounting unemployment and social disquiet. In response, the Labour government led by Harold Wilson in November 1967 devalued sterling to increase the competitiveness of British exports. At the same time the government, anxious to respond to increasing social disharmony, launched new forms of interventions in those areas thought to be worse affected by the country's changing fortunes. Alongside these the government commissioned a number of key reports to analyse the failure of the British welfare state to adequately provide for disadvantaged and marginal groups. These reports advocated more targeted intervention in predominately working-class areas. Some of the most significant were the Skeffington Report (HMSO, 1969) which recommended increased, if limited, public participation in planning; the Plowden Report (DES, 1967) which advocated a significant programme of positive discrimination in the primary education sector, including the development of local projects aimed at strengthening the relationship between the home, school and community; and the Fairbairn-Milson Report (DES, 1969) which suggested that youth work should develop a community perspective.

The rise of the CDPs

The establishment of the CDPs was part of a move by the state to play a more reflexive but at the same time an increasingly directive role in the life of local communities. In 1968 the government had launched the Urban Programme. This was believed by many to have been a response to Enoch Powell's 'Rivers of Blood' speech made in April that year predicting racial tension in British cities on a scale similar to that seen in the USA (Powell, 1968: 99). However, the Urban Programme was not restricted to areas considered to be prone to racial tension, partly for 'fear of provoking accusations of favoured treatment for immigrants' (Loney, 1983: 34). Rather it typically funded small scale projects, such as youth provision, child care facilities and advice centres in areas which had high levels of deprivation, defined in terms of social indicators relating to: unemployment; overcrowding; number of large families; poor environment; the disproportionate presence of immigrants; and the number of children in, or in need of care.

Although the Urban Programme proved popular at neighbourhood level where it provided funding and resources, there were a number of critics who highlighted the relatively small sums allocated to projects compared with the scale of the communities' problems. Benyon and Solomos (1987: 193) pointed out that the sums allocated to the Urban Programme were 'dwarfed' by the reductions in government funding to inner-city local authorities occurring at the same time.

The National CDP was part of a wider government initiative to address social disharmony and concerns that certain sections of the population were failing to successfully respond to the changing social and economic circumstances. There were a number of strands feeding into the process that led to the establishment of the CDPs. Amongst these was an awareness on the part of the Labour government that the numerically smaller Liberal Party was achieving success in local elections at their expense via campaigns based on 'community politics'. Indeed Peter Hain, now a Labour politician, but then a Liberal Party activist believed that community activity could be part of a process leading to a 'total transformation of society and a switch to a decentralised system' (Hain, 1976: 2).

In an attempt to regain the political initiative and extend strategies that would be electorally popular at both local and national level, whilst simultaneously dealing with concerns regarding poverty and participation, the government directed civil servants to examine the American *War on Poverty* programme. This was launched in January 1964 by the Democrat President Lyndon Johnson who in his State of the Union address promised to expand the federal government's role in social welfare programmes. Underpinning the Johnson reforms was an assumption that these would 'equip the poor to compete more effectively in the market place' (Loney, 1983: 27).

The instigators of British CDPs not only drew on the American experience but conferred with their US counterparts during the planning stage. In 1969 following these discussions and agreement on the design of the interventions, the Home Office sanctioned the launch of the National Community Development Project. Described in a Home Office press release as 'a major experiment in improving the social services for those most in need', four projects, later extended to 12, were to be established in areas with populations of between 3,000 and 15,000, that were experiencing significant social need. The projects were to be initially funded for a period of five years with the aim of discovering more successful ways of meeting need.

Each CDP was linked to a local authority that was required to provide 25 per cent of the funding and to a local university or polytechnic who was employed to undertake an evaluation of their performance. A central team based in the Home Office was established to co-ordinate the whole project and consider the lessons learnt in terms of future policy-making. The National CDP became at the time the largest action-research project ever funded by the British government. The major stated intention was to gather information about the impact of existing social policies and services and encourage innovation and co-ordination. The strong and explicit research focus and emphasis on social action was, according to Loney (1983: 3), a means of 'creating more responsive local services and of encouraging self help'. The project designers argued that the emergence and value of social science research methods of enquiry could be utilised to both better understand the host communities and assist in improving the delivery of local services.

CDPs and poverty

There were four key assumptions guiding the design of the National Community Development Project, all of which focus on poverty. These were:

1. That the causes of poverty were predominately individual: that the poor were primarily responsible for their own poverty because of their family patterns, their values and community structures;
2. That 'deviant' family structures caused poverty rather than that poverty caused 'deviant' family structures;
3. That 'poverty bred poverty' and an 'underprivileged' individual or family had an increased possibility of remaining poor. A key driver of the CDPs was for them to find ways of breaking the 'culture of poverty'. At the same time, the projects were to tackle institutional rigidity and insensitivity which the civil servants, who designed the projects, argued made many agencies irrelevant to the needs of the poor, and prevented effective inter-agency co-ordination to tackle specific problems;
4. That collecting intelligence and data in the 12 communities would prove valuable in identifying trends and changes in society relating to the transmission of poverty.

Loney (1983) claims that the when the Home Office created the CDPs the focus was on the micro rather than macro-level, with the programme directed at individuals and social service agencies. He argues that it was possible to identify a

strong relationship between the Home Office's 'conservative macro-theories of poverty and a programmatic focus on individuals' (1983: 68). It is interesting to note it was the Children's Department in the Home Office which conceived the CDPs and that within it traditional social work theories and practice rooted in individual, family and community pathologies were dominant.

John Greve (1969), a member of the team responsible for launching the CDPs, offered a list of indicators which could be used to assess the effectiveness of local projects. These reflected the social pathology assumptions noted above and included: reductions in rates of disease, debt, the number of children taken into care, juvenile delinquency and marital breakup.

How were the 12 areas selected?

According to official accounts, the areas selected to host the projects were identified by 'combining evidence of need with a judgement about the degree of commitment, professional skills and resources available locally' (CDA, 1968: 13: para. 13). However, as Loney (1983: 80) shows, scientific judgement was bypassed in preference for political pragmatism. For example in the first four projects one was to be located in Coventry where one of the constituencies was represented by the Secretary of State for Social Services, Richard Crossman. A second was located in Cardiff, represented by the Home Secretary James Callaghan, and a third in Southwark represented by Labour's Chief Whip, Bob Mellish. However, what is clear is that although political influence played a part, the 12 areas were chosen through a process of negotiation between the Home Office and local authorities (Payne and Smith, 1975).

Into the community

Once the local projects were launched the practitioners began using community development strategies to work with residents and local authorities to concentrate on their concerns and issues and to address the social needs identified by civil servants. Most projects opened neighbourhood advice centres which gave the workers an established and accepted public face in their area. They also gained local credibility by assisting in the development of non-contentious provision such as play groups. In all 12 areas the weakness of the labour market was identified by the workers as a problem for residents leading to individual and family poverty.

Each project was supported by a Steering Committee which included senior representatives from participating services such as housing, social services and education, plus representatives from central government and the voluntary sector. Local councillors, the project team leader and a representative from the university research team were also committee members. In time local residents joined these committees. As the projects developed it became clear there were growing divisions between the civil servants and those delivering and researching at the grass roots. Similarly divisions grew within and between projects. An inter-project working group was established to provide a forum to air these and progress the CDPs' work.

In 1973, four years into the projects, CDP personnel concluded that their main disquiet was with the philosophy and assumptions that had informed their inception. The following year they published an inter-project report which explained their position pointing out that:

> . . . *problems of multi-deprivation have to be redefined and reinterpreted in terms of structural constraint rather than psychological motivations, external rather than internal factors. The project teams were increasingly clear that the symptoms of disadvantage in their 12 areas cannot be explained adequately by any abnormal preponderance of individuals or families whose behaviour could be defined as 'pathological'. Even where social 'malaise' is apparent it does not seem best explained principally in terms of personal deficiencies so much as the product of external pressures in the wider environment.*

(CDP IIU, 1974: 8)

This move away from the four guiding assumptions, together with the increasing independence and the radicalism of the local projects prompted the Home Office to set up a management review. Since the launch of the CDPs, the Home Office had undergone a number of personnel changes and these combined with the sudden death of Derek Morell, the leading civil servant responsible for the projects, weakened the management structure. The review confirmed the move from original principles. It also highlighted the divided lines of accountability which had given the local projects increased room for manoeuvre and enabled the workers to develop and exercise their radical approaches. The review recommended a strengthening of the centralised aspects of the CDP including a return to the social pathology approach and the appointment of a Home Office approved editor for future joint inter-project publications.

Beginning of the end

The decision by the Home Office to undertake a management review, and then to implement the review's findings included freezing the recruitment of staff for seven months and subjecting the projects to a reassessment of their expenditure and a greater degree of central control. Clearly this indicated that radical views and style of neighbourhood intervention were no longer welcome. There is evidence that the review's findings demonstrated the government's declining interest in the CDPs and Alex Lyon, who entered the Home Office as Minister of State in 1974, later confirmed that the civil service was 'totally disillusioned with the CDPs' (Lyon, 1979: 24). In the wake of the review CDP staff made the decision that henceforth they would produce reports aimed mainly at the labour movement and community activists. By 1975 the Home Office had begun withdrawing finance and many local authorities proved unable or unwilling to continue their funding and consequently, the projects closed one-by-one.

What lessons can be learnt?

There are a number of inter-linking lessons to be learnt from this programme. The plethora of documents and reports produced by the individual CDP teams and the inter-project team provide us with a rich source of material which still has resonance today (a short list of key documents is offered at the end of this piece). The CDPs' radical critique of the government's housing, regional and industrial policies can also be used to better understand New Labour's reforms of the welfare state as well as those being introduced by the coalition government, particularly regarding the increasing role being given to private companies and capital.

In relation to community development, the CDP experience offers a number of lessons. Firstly, it is possible to develop initiatives that centre on the link between community organisations, the labour movement and the constantly evolving profit focused economic markets. The radical critique provided by the CDP workers and researchers shows it is impossible to have a detailed understanding of local issues without an appreciation of the wider forces shaping events. For example the Coventry CDP produced documentary evidence that the lack of investment in the motor industry in their city, leading to unemployment in the Hillfields area where the project was based, was due to trans-national corporations with headquarters elsewhere making decisions based solely on short term profit-focused goals (Benington, 1975). Over 35 years later the increasing impact of globalisation and the primacy of neo-liberal economics have made this analysis even more pertinent. This means it is now impossible to live in the UK without experiencing the outcome of fluid dynamic global economic relations and a fast changing social system that challenges traditional understandings of the local and the neighbourhood.

Secondly, the experience of the CDPs tells us a great deal about the space created by the contradictory pressure from the state's encouragement of voluntary effort and self-help. In the 1970s the CDPs were charged with supporting and encouraging local groups to assist in the delivery of services and recommend improvements in local and central government provision. This they did but not with the intention expected by the CDP designers. Instead the CDPs helped local residents develop self-help projects which in turn led them to put forward alternative approaches to the more traditional provision that had been offered. Since then a number of commentators, (see Gilchrist, 2009; Ledwith and Springett, 2010) have developed ideas which connect local practice by residents with larger social issues.

Thirdly, the CDPs illustrate the value of small-scale and often politically neutral projects. These provide valuable spaces to work alongside residents in a manner which can lead to discussions about wider issues. Whilst the extensive CDP literature offers a library of work that shows the importance of an understanding of the powerful forces impacting on neighbourhoods, it also provides case studies of work at the grass-roots level.

Finally we learn from the limits of the work. The CDPs were a reflection of their time. For example, there is little evidence in the reports that racism was considered an influence on community relations. Similarly there is a paucity of attention given to the role of women in community initiatives. These approaches were to be challenged and addressed by community development practitioners and writers from the late 1970s onwards and are now central concerns of an activity which centres on social justice and the need to challenge discrimination.

Conclusion

It is inconceivable today, when the UK has a far more sophisticated state, that a government would fund projects that transgressed their original brief. Certainly one suspects the government would now act swiftly to curtail projects that tried to move from incremental and small scale schemes focusing on mobilising communities to solve their own problems, to a position where state funded employees were articulating the development of alternative and politically radical views of poverty and deprivation. The New Deal for Communities introduced in 1998 is a recent example of government led and controlled intervention at neighbourhood level which did not countenance real participation by local people (Dinham, 2005; Popple, 2007). However we should take heart from the work of the CDPs as they provided us with a rich stream of theory, knowledge and practice that has helped us to better understand the need to promote forms of community development that have at their core the values of participation, empowerment, social inclusion and social justice. The CDPs explained and revealed the early impact of neo-liberal economic policies on British community life. Adherence to a neo-liberal approach to the economy and the scaling-down of the public sector is now the dominant view held by many governments. The UK is no exception for here successive governments have increasingly prioritised the private sector at the expense of the public sector, a prioritisation that has led to thousands of neighbourhoods experiencing severe economic and social disadvantage (Dominelli, 2007). Linking the global with the local is therefore as important now as it was when the CDPs alerted us to the fallout from the multi-faceted nature of international finance and capitalist enterprise.

Note

1   A central government led regeneration programme operating in 39 areas in England.

References

Benington, J. (1975) The Flaw in The Pluralist Heaven: Changing Strategies in the Coventry CDP. in R. Lees and G. Smith (eds.) *Action Research in Community Development*, London, Routledge and Kegan Paul.

Benyon, J. and Solomos, J. (1987) *The Roots of Urban Unrest*, Oxford, Pergamon Press.

CDA (1968) *Working Party on Community Development, Second Draft Report to Ministers* (Home Office Paper No. 13) London, Home Office.

Community Development Project Information and Intelligent Unit (1974) *The National Community Development Project: Inter-Project Report*, London, Home Office.

DES (1967) *Children and their Primary Schools. Report to the Central Advisory Council for Education, Volume 1 (Plowden Report)* London, HMSO.

DES (1969) *Youth and Community Work in the 1970s: Proposals by the Youth Service Development Council* (Fairbairn-Milson Report) London, HMSO.

Dinham, A. (2005) 'Empowerment or over-powered? The Real Experiences of Local Participation in the UK's New Deal for Communities' *Community Development Journal*, 40, 181–93.

Dominelli, L. (2007) *Communities in a Globalising World: Theory and Practice in Changing Contexts*, Aldershot, Ashgate.

Gilchrist, A. (2009) *The Well-connected Community: A Networking Approach to Community Development* (2nd edition) Bristol, Policy Press.

Greve, J. (1969) Community Development Project: research and evaluation in *Experiments in Social Policy and their Evaluation* (Report of an Anglo-American Conference held at Ditchley Park, Oxfordshire, 29–31 October) London, Home Office.

HMSO (1969) *People and Planning* (Skeffington Report) London, HMSO.

Hain, P. (1976) The Future of Community Politics. in P. Hain (ed.) *Community Politics*, London, John Calder.

Ledwith, M. and Springett, J. (2010) *Participatory Practice: Community-based Action for Transformative Change*, Bristol, Policy Press.

Loney, M. (1983) *Community Against Government: The British Community Development Project 1968–78*, London, Heinemann.

Lyon, A. (1979) A Labour View. in M. Loney and M. Allen (eds.) *The Crisis of the Inner City*, London, Macmillan.

Payne, J. and Smith, K. (1975) The Context of The Twelve Project Areas. in R. Lees and G. Smith (eds.) *Action Research in Community Development*, London, Routledge and Kegan Paul.

Popple, K. (2007) Community Development Strategies in the UK. in L. Dominelli (ed.) *Communities in a Globalising World: Theory and Practice in Changing Contexts*, Aldershot, Ashgate.

Powell, E. (1968) Text of speech delivered in Birmingham, 20 April 1968. *Race*, X 1, 80–104.

Selection of key CDP texts

CDP (1975) *The Poverty of the Improvement Programme*, London, CDP Information and Intelligence Unit.

CDP (1976) *Profits against Houses*, London, CDP Information and Intelligence Unit.

CDP (1976) *Whatever Happened to Council Housing?* London, CDP Information and Intelligence Unit.

CIS/CDP (1976) *Cutting the Welfare State (Who Profits)*, London, Counter Information Services and CDP.

CDP (1977) *The Cost of Industrial Change*, London, Community Development Project Inter-project Editorial Team.

CDP (1977) *Gilding the Ghetto: The State and the Poverty Experiments*, London, Community Development Project Inter-project Editorial Team.

CDP PEC (1979) *The State and the Local Economy*, London, CDP PEC and Publications Distributive Co-operative.

CHAPTER 11

From CYSA to CYWU: A Radical Journey Subverted

Tony Taylor

Study the historian, before you study the facts.

(Carr, 1964)

This chapter is an attempt to describe and interpret a tumultuous decade in the history of the Community and Youth Workers' Union (CYWU). No claims are made to being objective about these years from 1979 to 1989. After all I was a member of the cast playing out the drama. Indeed there were times when I assumed a principal role. Thus my version of the script is subjective. As Magri puts it, 'I cannot claim I was not there, I did not know' (2008: 62). But it is only my best effort at a memory. It is my hope that other memories of these days might be encouraged to emerge. My version is also explicitly political. I wish to revive for debate an account of this decade, which celebrates the creativity and imagination of a notable section of the membership. These women and men of differing ideological persuasions forged a powerful radical alliance, because of and in spite of their class, gender, race and sexuality, which transformed the organisation. At the same time, though, I am obliged to interrogate why this alliance imploded, in the face of what opposition and with what consequences.

As a prelude to this exploration I will begin with an impressionistic sketch of my first experience nationally, along with others, of the Community and Youth Service Association (CYSA), taken from a talk I gave at the old Leicester Polytechnic in 1984.

> *We are observing the goings on in the upstairs dining hall of a college in Birmingham. The year is 1980. Outside it is wet and murky, inside the lights shine down brightly on the Community and Youth Service Association's Annual Dinner, the highlight of its National Conference. The majority of those present are attired appropriately in suit and gown, whilst a sullen minority garbed in jeans and dungarees watch with mounting disbelief the unfolding proceedings. The top table, resplendent in their dinner jackets and chains, are hand-clapped rhythmically to their elevated seats. Hierarchy and protocol stifle*

the air. The pompous platform speeches riddled with sexist assumptions prove finally too much for the sensitivities of the scowling inhabitants of the corner table. We walk out, precipitating a row about and a severe ticking off for our infantile behaviour.

Suitably admonished we returned to our various workplaces, pondering what on earth we were doing in an organisation which oozed such an unexpected level of conservative and complacent conformity. Of course to judge CYSA so harshly on the basis of such an isolated, personal snapshot of its practices lacked a sense of contradiction. However, before exploring this further, I need to put our appearance at this gathering into context.

Youth work and the union: contested sites of practice

The journey into CYSA had begun a year earlier as Roy Ratcliffe and myself licked our wounds after being disciplined for supporting an insubordinate fledgling youth council. The irony, which will become apparent, is that we were members of the National Association of Local Government Officers (NALGO), who had given us precious little support. We determined to join the CYSA. With the backing of the newly formed Wigan Women Workers Group and a posse of part-timers from the authority's Qualifying Course in Youth Work, upon which we were tutors, we set up a local branch. The backdrop to this moment was one of a running battle over the previous five years about the purpose of youth work within the newly formed Metropolitan Borough of Wigan. Efforts to wrestle with the strengths and weaknesses of a non-directive approach had been resisted. The tension increased as we argued the necessity of engaging with issues of class, gender, race and sexuality. The fight to establish a Girls' Worker post was hard and long. The moral panic engendered by talking about homosexuality on the part-time worker training course led to the marvellous headline in the local paper, 'Seaside Sex Talks Set Tory Ladies Bristling'. The management of the service, although products of the post-Albermarle National College, where a liberal perspective was passionately promulgated, paid lip service to its ethos, but when backed into a corner sided with the forces of tradition. Plainly youth work in Wigan was a seriously contested site of practice. As it was, our first collective act as a new enthusiastic branch was to draft a local constitution expressing our commitment to equal opportunities and positive discrimination. This emphasis was rejected by CYSA's executive. Thence followed our experience at the national conference sketched earlier. If we had borne illusions, they were dispelled. CYSA was to be no haven of refuge, rather '. . . it was another front on which to struggle' (Ratcliffe, 1987: 3).

As we took a breath it was obvious that the CYSA would reflect the same tensions about practice that we were experiencing on the ground in our workplace.

There was a sense in which the full-time training of the time failed to engage with the competing ideological tendencies within the work. The emphasis in training was on a non-judgemental and non-directive methodology (Ewen, 1972). Many CYSA members saw themselves as neutral technicians in human relations, simply and naively doing their best for young people. To put it crudely, the National College didn't seem to do politics and neither it seemed, did the CYSA. As we journeyed back and forth from Wigan to Manchester, where the national office was situated, the contradictions continued to surface. We learnt that a group of women workers in London had left CYSA to join NALGO, whilst a number of black workers had resigned in order to form the Black Youth and Community Workers Association, frustrated respectively by CYSA's institutional sexism and racism (Ratcliffe, 1987: 15). Yet, in Sandra Leventon, CYSA boasted a woman Secretary General with a formidable reputation, although it is possible that this hard-earned status owed more to her proud record as a caseworker than to her skills as a collective organiser. Back in Wigan we were having furious arguments about whether it was legitimate for workers and young people to attend Anti-Nazi League festivals in the authority's mini-buses. Over in Manchester we seemed to be in the presence of an organisation that had sleepwalked through a decade of heightened social and political unrest.

Caucusing for change

In the months ahead of the 1981 CYSA conference a network of activists began to take shape. By twist of fate and in the absence of anyone else's interest, Roy Ratcliffe had become Editor of *Rapport*, the Association's monthly journal, and his transformation of its content, including a serious encounter with class, gender, race and sexuality, was engendering a growing sense of solidarity. This togetherness was enhanced through the organisation by the Wigan CYSA branch of a two-day gathering at the Abraham Moss Centre, *Youth Work and the Crisis*, which sought to bring attention to the radical analysis of the Enfranchisement Project at the National Youth Bureau, to the critical work of Bernard Davies, exemplified by his landmark text, *In Whose Interests?* (1979) and to the wider debate about being 'in and against the state' (London-Edinburgh Return Group, 1980). That, in those days, we would put one another up on makeshift mattresses in spare rooms, travelling far and wide, added to the collective feeling.

Whilst Doug Nicholls in his sweeping history of the organisation notes that 'there were stirrings of a new radical life' at the CYSA conference itself, he glosses over the enormous political energy and tension underlying the convulsion. Blandly he remarks that 'historically the Association formed its first Women's Caucus, a self-organised group for women only, proposed by Julie Hart and seconded by

Frankie Williams' (Nicholls, 2009: 106). It was not at all so straightforward. As I recall the detail, on the Saturday evening a group of women workers frustrated by their marginalisation called a women only meeting to consider the situation. The next morning in an unparalleled move they proposed a suspension of standing orders in order to debate a resolution, arguing for their right to caucus openly and formally. Astonishment rippled through the hall. The proposal was opposed vehemently on the grounds that the women were asking for preferential treatment. The following discussion was intense, but to the great credit of the conference, more open than much of its Executive, the suspension was agreed. The argument raged back and forth. In a moment of inspiration Leslie Silverlock from the chair suggested a tea break, whilst everyone calmed down. As the women pondered what to do next and what to call themselves, Sue Atkins recalls Roy Ratcliffe crawling between rows of chairs to suggest, 'Why not a caucus?' The reply was, 'Why not indeed!' Apocryphal though this tale might be, in the end, amidst much anxiety and by a slender majority, the conference supported the birth of the Women's Caucus. I must recognise too that this historic outcome gives the lie to exaggerating the reactionary character of the Association. On the Executive the aforementioned Leslie Silverlock, the ever sharply dressed President and the often more casual Phil Coughlin, the Honorary General Secretary, were supportive and in the body of the hall over half of those present stood up to be counted.

In the ensuing *Rapport* the editorial proclaimed:

> . . . *the Women's Caucus is the collective response of women in the CYSA to the domination of men within the organisation. That this has been formally recognised by the highest decision making body of CYSA – its national conference brings credit and stature to our organisation. We owe our thanks to the Women's Caucus for bringing our attention to this principle (of caucusing) and reminding us of its existence.*
>
> (*Rapport*, May 1981)

The ferment resulting from this victory bubbled through the rest of the year. The traditionalists complained within *Rapport* about disruptive elements, whilst the Caucus deepened its roots, holding a conference attended by over 70 women. In its report for the 1982 conference the women noted:

> *Members at the AGM argued against a women's caucus. 'Have a standing committee they told us, then we can fit you into the present system.' But the present system was not working – alternatives needed to be explored and a women's caucus can respond to the demands of women workers in the field rather them responding to ready made rules and procedures.*
>
> (*Rapport*, January 1982)

It is necessary to underline a number of points about this historic breakthrough which are missing from Nicholls' somewhat cursory reference.

1. The challenge to sexism in the Association had come from below and in an important sense from outside of the organisation's culture.
2. The notion of explicit and open caucusing as a means of articulating the views of those with less influence and power was a practical and political creation. It was not artificially imposed.
3. The process illustrated that the hierarchical structure of the Association could be challenged and defeated if ordinary members organised to take control of 'their' organisation.

Caucusing was catching on. At the 1981 national training conference held at Stoke Rochford, 40 of those present met independently to consider the idea of forming a Trade Union Caucus. This proposal was inspired by the motion to change the name of CYSA to CYWU, which had not been put to allow wider debate. Our pluralist alliance focused its attention on how best to confirm the organisation's commitment to challenging exploitation and oppression. Its members left the weekend agreeing to undertake a range of tasks before the 1982 AGM and proud to belong to a caucus, which had met in front of open doors, honest about its intentions. Certainly Nicholls recognises that 'there was a feeling of excitement in the air', but he fails conspicuously to mention the organisational form into which this enthusiasm was channelled. He uses a peculiar but informative analogy, explaining 'the spirit of 68 and Woodstock were coming to the Association, late but better late than never' (Nicholls, 2009: 109). As far as I recall, none of us were, in Joni Mitchell's words, 'stardust trying to get back to the garden'. Our feet were firmly on the ground. Much more appropriately he might have recognised it was the spirit of the Women's Peace Camp at Greenham and the struggle of Asian women workers at Grunwicks that was quickening our stride.

The 1982 AGM received an unprecedented number of resolutions witness to the vibrancy of the period. The TU Caucus worked overtime to draw up its advice to the membership on how we viewed specific resolutions and to organise its own interventions. The Women's Caucus met both separately and as a partner in the TU Caucus itself. As a result of this collective diligence the Association awoke with a new name, the Community and Youth Workers' Union, and a rack of radical policies. Concerned to maintain the momentum we moved a successful resolution setting up a working party to review the constitution in the light of the dramatic changes.

Opposition to the transformation was not going to go away, which was perfectly in order. Except that this resistance chose to organise itself very much in secret and behind closed doors. The progress of the constitution working party was far from serene, especially as Keith Bell, the Secretary General, seemed to take every opportunity to muddy the waters. Trying to amend a bureaucratic constitution in the name of democracy proved deeply frustrating. The framework for the union's activities was provided by the recommendations of the Glassman Report, referred to as 'a corporate strategy consultancy', which were accepted in February 1973. In fact, the said report was the MBA thesis of a student at the Cranfield School of Management. Within the document the author refers to a process wherein the officers of CYSA were asked to draw an organisational chart. 'All drew vertical, hierarchical charts with the national officers at the top and the members at the bottom – except in one case where the members were omitted altogether' (quoted in Ratcliffe, 1987: 16). This managerial structure and its advocates were proving to be a major obstacle to the challenge of preparing a coherent alternative.

In the midst of our exasperation, the good humour of the Chair, George Neely, served us well, but his quip that 'he was adamant that the first draft was scribbled hastily by himself on the back of a fag packet' (Nicholls, 2009: 115) was a typical jest. The first draft of a complete would-be new constitution was put together by Roy Ratcliffe and myself, largely on the way back from yet another abortive meeting in the metropolis – a veritable Wigan-London Day Return Group! Whilst worried about being seen as presumptuous, we took succour in a belief that our suggestions flowed from the organisation's collective experience over the preceding few years. Neither did we hide the fact that our perspective was informed by our critical engagement with both Marxism and feminism. To our relief our proposal was not seen as pretentious by the working group. It was welcomed eagerly and animated argument ensued. Courtesy of Roy's joy, a state-of-the-art word processor, and fortified by endless cups of Viennese coffee flavoured with fig, our draft went through nine stages of revision. The final document was 30 pages in length but only because each and every proposal was supported by the working group's rationale. Such detail was felt to be crucial. There was no desire to hoodwink the membership into acceptance of something they didn't quite understand. However the desire of the working group to circulate the explanation to all the membership was refused on the grounds of cost. This failure to explain fully to the membership, present and future, the thinking behind this radical constitution haunted us immediately back in 1982, bedevilled its adoption in ensuing years, and allows it to be dismissed nowadays as the offspring of 'a romantic mentality of utopian ultra democracy' (2009: 148).

What were its utopian essentials?

1. It turned upside down the previous arrangements. Executive and managerial power was replaced by a democratic structure within which power resided in those below, with the membership.

2. True to the classic, usually ignored labour movement demand, it rendered all official positions, including the full-time national post, subject to election, accountability and recall. As a challenge to traditional trade union norms, the full-time National Organiser was not an employee. He or she was simply privileged to be the paid member of the union's leadership, remunerated on the same pay scale and conditions as the membership itself. This was a response to the long-standing concern within the labour movement that its leaders and officials had grown into a separate bureaucratic caste with interests and lifestyles very different than those who had elected or appointed them. In a small, but significant way we sought to break from this corrosive legacy. In addition the Organiser could only hold the position for three years before a further election took place. This was intended to strengthen democratic control, to guard against the widespread phenomenon of General Secretaries seeming to hold office for life and to extend/ rotate leadership in the union.
3. It affirmed the centrality of the branch and the caucus for the time being as the organisational lifeblood of the organisation.
4. At the national level it subverted the idea of a National Executive Committee (NEC) which knows better than the membership, with a National Organising and Coordinating Committee (NOCC) which was to be the conscience and servant of the rank and file.

From its appearance it struck terror into the bureaucratically inclined of all political persuasions. However it was initially the Right wing in the union who kicked off a concerted effort to prevent its adoption. The Special General Meeting held in Coventry was sabotaged by a walkout led by the Nottinghamshire branch. Nevertheless those left (85 representatives from 27 branches) threw themselves into a two-day debate. At the end, an informal vote was proposed. Overwhelmingly supported, the new arrangements were affectionately dubbed 'the Coventry Constitution'.

1983: A new dawn?

Reflecting the widespread approval of the constitution, it was to be proposed and seconded by Lesley Silverlock and Phil Coughlin, the union's chief officers. But this moment had to wait as the Nottinghamshire branch had tabled a complete alternative. Yet again the TU Caucus and the Women's Caucus worked tirelessly across the two days, especially as a host of amendments needed to be discussed, most of which were intended to undermine the philosophy and intent of the new proposals. As Ratcliffe notes,

> ... looking tired and drawn our members ... made their way to the Conference Hall ... when it came to the debate on the full document there

was very little to be said and even less energy to say it. When the President called for the vote, it was akin to an exhausted anti-climax.

(1987: 11)

Nevertheless it was a notable achievement. Grass roots organisation in the form of open caucusing had transformed the outlook and structure of the former CYSA. And, knowing this and trusting one another, many of those involved agreed to form a Broad Left Caucus to continue the work.

1984–1985: Dusk threatens

Knackered though we were, we exuded optimism. The membership had embraced the constitution and set up an Amalgamation Working Party. Clearly they were able to juggle with different scenarios at one and the same time, radicalising their union, whilst exploring the possibility of merger, if appropriate and sense making with a larger organisation. What we required at this point was a period of consolidation as we tangled with the dilemmas of putting principles into practice. We needed some time and space. This was never to be. At the national committee level the full-time official backed by key officers, such as the President, Allen Clarke and the Treasurer, Gina Ingram, imagined obstacles where none existed, and seemed to drag their feet at every opportunity. From the Left, Doug Nicholls claims to be the first person to articulate public discontent with the way things were. In an article, 'Class first for CYWU', he 'criticised the new constitution for making the union resemble more a community association of loosely federated worthy causes, or a pressure group than a union.' In the same vein, writing on behalf of the Coventry branch he repeated, 'one of the consequences of the peculiar combination of interest group politics and uppity professionalism that prevails in CYWU is the evident lack of concern for our pay campaign' (Nicholls, 126: 129). These are early, thinly veiled attacks on caucusing, which do a disservice in particular to the Women's and Part-Time Workers caucuses, which were hardly 'worthy causes'. As for class politics, my 1985 Chair's report to the membership, whilst tub-thumpingly Trotskyist in tone, proclaimed:

> *we require a trade union which fights tooth and nail over the basic issues of pay and conditions, but one which asserts in the same breath that the only lasting solution is the control of society in the name of social need rather than private greed.*

(Quoted in Nicholls, 2009: 128)

In agreement with Nicholls we wanted to break from a parasitism on the teachers' fight for better pay. Ironically, though, it was the National Union of Teachers' (NUT) interference in our affairs that was central to preventing NOCC from getting on with its daily business.

Intent internally on crushing its own dissidents, the Inner London Teachers Association and Socialist Teachers Alliance, the NUT was not happy about the radical noises emerging from CYWU, a constituent Association. The NUT bureaucracy declared the constitution unacceptable and too political, hinting heavily that, unless changes were made, they would pull the financial plug. A troika, a very secret caucus of Allen Clarke, the president, Gina Ingram, the Treasurer, and Geoff Eagle, the Honorary General Secretary, saw this as the opportunity to overthrow what had been achieved by open caucusing. In a coup planned to deliver us from our democratic sins, they seized the pages of *Rapport* to inform the membership that we would collapse if the NUT was not heeded immediately (*Rapport*, February, 1986). At a NOCC meeting in Sheffield attended by over 60 members the union called the bluff and held its nerve. Those who turned up to defend the organisation, were overwhelmingly drawn from the ranks of the best organised branches and the caucuses. The very forces which had transformed the union, came together to save the organisation. An interim NOCC was elected with Bernard Davies as President, myself, the Honorary General Secretary, Roy Ratcliffe (Treasurer), Gill Millar (Editor of *Rapport*), Sue Atkins (Education Officer), Roger Dibben (Chair of Salaries and Tenure), Julia Lyford (Caucus Liaison Officer), and members Deborah Ball, Gary McAlister, Carol Stone, Sue Morgan, Margaret Gale, May Jenkins, Frankie Williams and Helen Voller. Nicholls' analysis of these exhausting months is confusing and contradictory. On the one hand he acknowledges that a few dedicated individuals saved the Union from a bitter end, noting the exceptional efforts of Roy Ratcliffe 'who moved temporarily from Wigan to Tring, to effectively rescue the infrastructure and democratic heart of the union' (2009: 125). On the other, almost in the same breath, he argues that the union needed to be returned to its members and rescued from the clutches of the 'aficionados of the political debates', who were splitting the union. Evidently 'for the majority the identity crisis had gone on long enough and a move to more solid ground was needed' (2009: 131). In contrast my best recollection is that we, 'aficionados', were doing our damnedest to restore solid ground by producing a balanced budget, by putting in hours above and beyond the call of duty and by setting up the Inquiry (led by Bernard Davies) into the tragicomic farce. The crisis was not down to a collective personality disorder or a lack of trade union discipline, but to political skulduggery. In fact the splitters had fled, having resigned, with over £6,000 missing from the union's slender coffers, paid as unapproved severance to the former full-time official, Keith Bell (*Rapport*, Feb 1986; May 1986).

THE JOURNAL OF THE COMMUNITY & YOUTH WORKERS UNION

110 Western Road, Tring, Herts.
Tel: 044 282 2905.

FEB 86

CYWU - ALIVE & WELL!

Many members will obviously be worried by the statements made in the personal mailing they've received from Geoff Eagle, Allen Clarke and Gina Ingram. This mailing is issued by the NOCC to put the record straight and to assure members that CYWU is alive and well, and continues to function as the only specialist union for youth and community workers.

EVENTS LEADING TO PRESENT SITUATION.

The NOCC meeting on 23rd December approved a budget and agreed unanimously not to take any action which would lead to overspending. The treasurer assured the NOCC that she would do nothing outside NOCC and National Conference policy. She confirmed that she would comply with the meeting's decisions, otherwise she would resign.

On January 2nd members of NOCC discovered, by indirect channels, that the Secretary General was no longer working for CYWU, and that severance pay of £6,500 had been paid out from CYWU funds, without the knowledge of the NOCC or the membership. Clause 11(c) of the constitution states that payments outside the budget must be approved by NOCC or National Conference. At the same time we heard of the resignations of the President, Treasurer and Hon. Gen. Sec.. These events came to light just before the January Rapport mailing was due to go out. The Editor discovered that the personal mailing received by members was intended to be distributed at the same time as Rapport.

Since that time a vast amount of work has been undertaken. Roy Ratcliffe has spent his holiday in Tring trying to get to the bottom of things at the National Office. NOCC members have contacted NUT's legal department and NUT executive members, and have been reassured that there is no immediate danger to our position within their union. Roy has come up with a series of budget projections for 1986 which would leave us with a surplus at the end of the year. Branches have been contacted and urged to attend the special NOCC meeting on 14th January.

SPECIAL NOCC.

This meeting was attended by an unprecedented number, over 60 people representing 32 branches. The strength of feeling and depth of confusion experienced by members was impressed upon the NOCC, and the level and intensity of debate at the meeting reflected the committment to CYWU.

BUDGET.

Roy Ratcliffe presented a financial report in two parts, firstly the present position which shows up to have over £16,000 in the bank, although the bulk of this money is due to be paid to NUT as 1985 subscriptions, plus £700 which had come in from subscriptions by 13th January. He also presented budget options for 1986, based on membership figures ranging from 1,000 to 1,650 (membership at the end of 1985 was over 2,000). After a lengthy debate this budget was accepted. By adhering to this budget CYWU will end the year out of debt and with a surplus of over £3,000. Clearly, without the necessity to pay the salary for a full-time official there is considerably more financial flexibility. The salary for an elected National Organiser has been budgeted

The alliance implodes

Certainly though, a critical moment was nearing, which is best understood by taking a step back. Across 1984 and 1985 the Broad Left Caucus had grown as a diverse, tolerant and lively entity, retaining the support of many feminists within the Women's Caucus. I remember with much affection woman, man and beast huddled together, 'sleeping over' at the St Michaels Centre in Deptford, still arguing the toss, irritating our fellow passengers, as we journeyed home together in a packed carriage from London to Sheffield. Such was our solidarity that in the immediate aftermath of the manufactured crisis we discussed and provisionally agreed to run a slate of 15 people for election to the NOCC. This idea was a frustrated response to the previous few years, within which our efforts to stabilise the union had been constantly subverted by what we saw as conspiratorial conservative attacks on the constitution. It would also provide a collective source of energy, given that many of us were feeling pretty run down from our exertions. However, as the consequences of the proposal sank in, disquiet surfaced. There was a threatening aspect to its 'vote for all of us or none of us' slogan. It implied that if you were on the Broad Left slate you were under Broad Left manners. Where did this leave other reference points – the branches and, most sensitively, the Women's Caucus itself? Wasn't there a hint of hubris at its heart? At an emotional meeting in Chesterfield the dilemmas became polarised and nine women withdrew from the slate.

Thus at the 1986 AGM in Lancaster the Broad Left Slate, which had been at its inception an expression of perhaps the most influential grouping in the union, was reduced to just six people, the expression of a self-styled revolutionary minority. Looking back we did have choices. At the time, several of us felt strongly that we wished to articulate more clearly our eclectic mix of anarchist and Marxist ideas. We could have done so by withdrawing from the elections, whilst continuing to be activists at a local and national level. Or, given that five of the Slate were elected, we could have swallowed our pride, recognising the faith in us expressed by the membership, and have taken up our positions in a spirit of reconciliation with the Women's Caucus. Fascinatingly Nicholls makes no reference to these events, which were by no means inconsequential in the scheme of things. On the surface, the situation would seem to offer him a heaven sent opportunity to pour scorn on our self-indulgent sectarianism. Unfortunately though. this would also mean revealing, despite his claim the membership desired 'a new trade union determination', that we had retained their confidence. Two of us had been voted in as President and Treasurer.

In my view our arrogant decision not to take up these key roles and to retreat into a critical opposition was deeply mistaken. Without doubt it cost us the goodwill and support of the overwhelming number, who had backed us. They felt let down and spurned. By absenting ourselves from the leadership we abandoned what Ratcliffe calls 'an alliance of women and men organised around the politics of feminism, socialism and anti-racism' (1987: 6). Shortly after the conference we announced formally our intention to set up the Socialist Caucus, which was accepted. Our claim was that during our self-inflicted exile we were seeking to be both supportive and critical of those we dubbed condescendingly 'the social democratic feminists' on NOCC in the face of the tightening grip of 'the Stalinists', our characterisation of the group around Nicholls and Orley Thorne. Whilst our observations were often insightful and always in defence of conference decisions, it is doubtful whether the patronising nature of our advice was of much use to the likes of Sue Atkins, Alima Sonne, Carol Stone, Julia Lyford and Gill Millar, struggling to develop a pragmatic consensus. Our uncertainty about our tactics led to fissures in our own ranks. Both Roy Ratcliffe and Andy Smart departed, citing our slide into a comfort zone of collective smugness. Echoing this criticism Sue Atkins, in a turn of phrase that can only raise a chuckle, is quoted as saying we were a bunch of 'shites in whining armour!' (Nicholls, 2009: 139).

In the ensuing period, the NOCC sought to function in difficult circumstances, not the least of which were the palpable lack of resources to do the job. In addition their efforts were clouded by differing estimates of how to handle the relationship with the NUT. The events of late 1985 had sown anxiety, prompting contrived attacks on the constitution in the name of necessity. The cry was 'to have a future, we must pacify the NUT!' In particular the attacks on caucusing became ever more distorted and aggressive. Rather than being seen as the dynamic and fluid form which had inspired the creation of the CYWU, caucusing was depicted as divisive and manipulative.

Caucusing recalled

With this in mind it is worth reminding ourselves of the original rationale for caucusing in the Coventry constitution. The formulation was that 'any group of like-minded individuals should have the right to caucus openly in the union as a key element in its internal democracy'. This was explicitly a challenge to the behind-the-scenes closet caucusing typically undertaken by those within the trade union leadership and bureaucracy. It was inherently democratic.

We were clear that this formulation supported the birth of caucuses based on oppression. In a rewriting of history, Nicholls claims that the original constitution spoke of state oppression (2009: 115). This is mistaken. The CYWU created women's, black, lesbian and gay caucuses, primarily to challenge prejudice within the organisation itself. The constitution embraced also the formation of caucuses around class exploitation, such as the Broad Left and socialist groupings. Yet it could also accommodate the particular concerns of less powerful constituencies such as part-time or rural workers. So too it could engage with long-term and short-term caucusing, for example, a group wanting just to organise around a particular policy in the months leading up to the national conference. The beauty of the structure was that it was self-policing. The test of the seriousness of a proposal to caucus was whether in reality its supporters had the commitment and discipline to organise in a transparent way, reporting regularly to the membership. Indeed, knowing that the road was not easy, we had created the post of Caucus Liaison Officer to support and facilitate the journey. As to whether a caucus was recognised or indeed aspired to a place on the NOCC, the Conference always had the last word.

This is perhaps the moment too to deal with the issue of formal committees and the regional structure, which was forever being pushed back to the fore. The rationale behind the constitution made clear that it was not in principle opposed either to a Women's Committee or to a regional framework per se. However it argued that such committees and regional bodies had to be based on the existence of an active and vibrant membership, expressed in strong branches and energetic caucusing. Without these ingredients committees and regional bodies were likely to become the self-serving fiefdoms of the few. Finally, if formal committees and regional committees were to be agreed, the right to caucus would remain crucial as a check on any tendency to bureaucratise and as a means for unity in diversity to flower. Thus, whilst a Women's Committee might emerge, this would never mean the end of the possibility of caucuses of Christian women or radical feminists et al pursuing their democratic right to self-organise within the union.

Old and new waves?

During the period of our self-imposed exile from the leadership of the union, NOCC was faced with organising the election of the National Organiser, a full-time post directly answerable to the membership. In his history Nicholls feels moved to identify the politics of his opponents. Pedro Connor and Julia Lyford are said to be radical feminist, anarcho-syndicalist in inclination, whilst Malcolm Peach is branded a maverick, window-cleaning member of the Communist Party of Great Britain. Meanwhile he characterises himself as nothing but a mere bread and butter trade unionist, healing the divisions of the past (2009: 135). This is disingenuous. His intervention into the union's affairs was informed unavoidably by his allegiance to the politics of the Communist Party of Britain (Marxist-Leninist) or CPB(M-L) who, to say the least, would have been uneasy about the 'libertarian' direction being taken by the CYWU.

It is revealing to note that his election address contained no reference to his political misgivings about the whole structure of CYWU. Indeed he emphasised that 'organising the whole workforce into one union is an urgent necessity' (*Rapport*, March 1987) which suggested a measure of sympathy with merger that was not forthcoming. In truth it is sobering to reflect that for the second time in less than two years the union faced a full-time official at odds with the democratically agreed constitution. His feelings about the post itself are reflected in a retrospective, rising tirade about the intolerable position of the National Organiser with its uncertain tenure, inappropriate pay and title. Significantly Nicholls explains that 'the professional authority required by a leading officer within the labour movement was simply lacking in the National Organiser' (2009: 134). Someone with such a demeaning title would not be welcomed or respected in the corridors of Transport House.

Nicholls records the impact of his coming to post immodestly, 'five months after the election and as a testament to the membership's renewed faith in its organisation, the membership barrier of 2000 was broken' (2009: 137) and 'the union started to motor ahead' (2009: 136). The narrative is becoming familiar. We are to believe that CYWU had lost its bearings, its rudderless leadership fixated on identity politics, utterly oblivious to issues of pay and conditions. Thus we are told that 'there was a danger that the baby would be thrown out with the bath water in the name of a radical change'; that 'a new wave of politics led by a loose network of branches' (2009: 137) was prioritising the centrality of the JNC and a campaign for regradings; and that the new Organiser was taking upon himself the task of breaking down the idea that 'branches were autonomous free-floating entities with no obligation to the national union' (2009: 141). Meanwhile, in the murk of reality, the remaining stalwarts of 1985 on NOCC were still battling on, working hard locally as well as nationally and utterly committed to the JNC. They were resilient and very grateful for the arrival of fresh faces, of which there were few. In fact vacancies were the norm. If the new wave was coming, it had not arrived. Even those of us, who could be criticised, as we have seen, for abdicating from the leadership, were in the forefront of every JNC lobby, conspicuous by our presence at every national meeting and amongst the most militant in resisting management attacks on our professional autonomy, as in the Derbyshire branch.

Nevertheless it must be conceded that the old wave was crashing on the rocks. Further evidence of the collapse in the relationship between the former members of the Broad Left can be seen in a number of incidents. In 1987 at Reading, Sue Atkins, as a President searching for a middle way, labelled us 'constitutional fundamentalists' for arguing against a number of concessions to the NUT. By this time we were not listening to one another. Our objection was not fetishistic. Quite simply we believed there was no need to make concessions before it was absolutely necessary and so it proved. The following year in Leeds during a debate on amalgamation, Malcolm Ball was booed for arguing that he thought of himself first as a local government worker and only then as a youth worker. Then the following day in a discussion on 'Irish racism', a black caucus member, Bob Evans, argued that caucusing should only be allowed on the basis of 'felt' or state oppression, implying illogically that the Socialist Caucus ought to be disenfranchised. To our consternation influential members of the Women's Caucus seemed to support this incoherent revision. In the end the conference let matters lie, but the last vestiges of trust between ourselves and our former allies seemed to be ebbing away. To add insult to injury the Women's Caucus moved a resolution in support of acquiescing to the NUT. In our eyes they were forgetting their own history, their seminal role in overturning the status quo.

A last throw of the dice

Whatever the depth of our self-indulgence or our capacity for making mistakes, we proved capable of self-criticism. More and more convinced that the political priority was to unite the workforce, we threw ourselves back into the centre of the union's activities. In late 1987 I was returned to NOCC as an ordinary member from the Derbyshire branch. In theory an Amalgamation Working Party (AWP) was exploring alternatives in the light of the end of the agreement with NUT in December 1988. In practice it had been put on ice. The months slid by and despite three years of supposed negotiations with the NUT, uncertainty reigned. Finally at the 1988 Leeds conference it was agreed that the AWP ought to be given the kiss of life. With time in short supply, I became a member of the AWP and was delegated to revive the NALGO option. In a frantic few months a resuscitated two-phase proposal was placed on the table. The framework envisaged a partnership period of one to five years, within which CYWU continued to conduct its own affairs, whilst working towards a mutually agreed integration into the larger union. It was noted that 'not only, for example, would women and black workers be able to organise autonomously within a Youth and Community Work Section, they would be able to participate in NALGO's national women and black workers' structures' (*Rapport*, October 1988). In a notable about turn, which illustrated the strength of the proposal, NOCC voted 13 to 7 in favour of recommending the NALGO package.

At the 1988 December Special Conference itself, Doug Nicholls presented the NUT case, Sue Atkins the NATFHE deal, whilst I spoke to the NALGO option. I did not speak on behalf of the Socialist Caucus as alleged (Nicholls, 2009: 146), but as the delegated member of the AWP and the NOCC. My speech was clearly underwhelming and the conference voted by 60 per cent to 40 per cent to stay with the NUT. I suspect we had blown the NALGO chance two years earlier on the night in Lancaster when we refused to take high office. As for the argument on the day, the National Organiser is correct to say that it was well-argued, emotional, tearful and exhausting (2009: 146). He crosses the line though when he claims that after the vote the NALGO official and EC member organised a meeting of NALGO supporters 'to plan a mass migration into NALGO' (2009: 147). In fact, supporters of the NALGO offer did meet prior to the debate with Dave Prentiss and Jean Geldart present. Within the discussion Malcolm Ball did not endear himself to these two individuals, warning all those present not to put their trust in the NALGO bureaucracy. As for post-conference, a small meeting did occur without any NALGO officials intervening. Nicholls is right to note that 'only a tiny handful moved'. For our part a mass exodus was never planned. Those of us in the Socialist Caucus resigned, explaining our reasons for doing so in a letter to the President, which was never published. In arguing that we were committed to strengthening the Youth and Community Work Section's relationship with all other local government and voluntary sector workers in NALGO, we expressed a hope 'that our separate paths might cross again in the future'. We did not leave lightly, especially in the face of the eloquent plea to stay made by Dave Sternberg and Sue Wyatt (*Rapport*, January 1989).

Before concluding I hope the reader will forgive one last moment of putting the record straight. Nicholls goes on to argue that NALGO attempted an offensive against both JNC and CYWU. It blocked CYWU's TUC application and in his words:

> . . . *became fond, through former members of the CYWU Socialist Caucus of leafleting CYWU Conferences, of telling delegates they would be better off on the lower pay and shorter holidays of APT&C and that JNC was elitist and reactionary.*

(Nicholl, 2009: 147)

In truth we had no truck with NALGO's petty blocking of CYWU's TUC application. We did attempt to hold one fringe meeting at the CYWU conference in Morecambe to debate whether APT&C had any merits as a unifying pay scale, particularly in relation to part-time workers. We handed out leaflets in a light hearted way, offered free beer and nobody turned up. The suggestion that we did so at the behest of the NALGO hierarchy is comical, but telling. It tends to confirm our fear at the time, expressed in our resignation letter, 'if we stay, continuing to propose our sense of affairs, we will be accused of being undemocratic and undermining the union'. This seemed to be in nobody's interest.

Conclusion

Underlying all these comings and goings is a profoundly serious question. In the struggle for democracy and social justice, how should we organise and on the basis of what ideas and principles? For Doug Nicholls the answer is clear and his version of history seeks to justify his response. His perspective reflects Reg Birch's analysis of British trade unionism. The charismatic founder of the CPB(M-L) believed one-sidedly that the trade unions were innately 'organs of class struggle with no other purpose' (Birch, 1971). Further he stressed that a central task was to build distinctive craft or professional unions. Nicholls has worked single-mindedly to ensure that CYWU followed this particular path. As part of this process it was crucial that the CYWU reverted to a time-honoured, hierarchical way of organising with a General Secretary at the helm and so it came to pass. In tune with the Party's hostility to what it dubs an ultra-left or liberal establishment obsession with gender, race and sexuality (*Workers*, September 2009) it was vital to undermine the right to caucus. All of these interventions were undertaken in the name of returning the CYWU to a British working class politics. However the variety of Marxist-Leninist theory underpinning this strategy is closed, immune in its supposed scientific confidence from criticism. Whatever the rhetoric about listening to the workers, to the membership, the leadership is an enlightened vanguard. However, it must be allowed that in the case of CYWU the graft, discipline and touch of ruthlessness demanded by this form of 'communist' politics has won the day. As a way of rationalising the overall history of the union Nicholls now paints a picture of unremitting progress, 'Seventy Years of Struggle', ruptured contradictorily only by the figures and events of the 1980s. The caucuses that transformed the organisation are turned gradually into a fictitious 'enemy within'.

As it was we proved perhaps to be our own worst enemies. Initially our effort to root a political alliance in the right to self-organise was open and imaginative. We were trying to create prefigurative ways of being together, of being both supportive and critical across our political differences. Feminism jostled with Marxism and Anarchism, Black politics rubbed shoulders with sexual politics. Our proposals were works in progress, subject to question. Our vision of the union was not hierarchical or bureaucratic. We were the authors of an authentically democratic constitution. So too we aspired to a way of organising that was inclusive not exclusive; that envisaged youth and community workers, social workers, caretakers and cleaners, clerks and administrative staff standing arm in arm in solidarity. But maintaining a sense of purpose, whilst being harassed from Right, Left and Centre, proved too much. To different degrees we succumbed to the pressures and retreated into our own closed ways of seeing things, typified by the gross error of the Slate and the backtracking on the principle of caucusing. And we were swimming against the tide. By the end of the 80s the labour movement was in disarray, whilst the social movements were withdrawing into collaboration with the state and turning against each other. This was mirrored perhaps in the collapse of our own relationships with each other. Nevertheless we were right to try. At our boldest we were pioneers. Learning from our mistakes we must renew our commitment to forging alliances of unity in diversity, knowing there are no guarantees that we will get it right. As Selma James, the remarkable Marxist feminist provisionally put it, nigh on 35 years ago, in the conclusion of her classic, *Race, Sex and Class*:

> *How the working class will ultimately unite organisationally, we don't know. We do know that up to now many of us have been told to forget our own needs in some wider interest which was never wide enough to include us. And so we have learnt by bitter experience that nothing unified and revolutionary will be formed until each section of the exploited will have made its own autonomous power felt.*
>
> *Power to the sisters and therefore to the class.*

(James, 1975)

Postscript

As for the contemporary situation on the ground within youth work, the workforce remains divided, split now across UNISON and UNITE. For different reasons and in differing ways, both sides of the 1980s divide got it wrong. Our paramount goal should have been to bring the workers under one roof and no amount of historical revision rids us of the responsibility to reflect critically on our failure to make this happen. In the end we cannot escape the fundamental dilemma – we can only create democracy by 'doing' democracy, in whatever and whichever place we find ourselves.

Acknowledgements

Whilst this is very much a personal interpretation, my thanks are due to Sue Atkins, Malcolm Ball, Tania de St Croix, Bernard Davies, Tim Price and Marilyn Taylor for their critical comments. I hope that some of their alternative memories might emerge in the future. Finally in the early part of the chapter I lean heavily on the notes I made for a lecture back in the 90s, which drew enormously on a pamphlet written by Roy Ratcliffe. Sadly, despite Roy emptying the loft, this important recollection in its entirety has been lost.

References

Birch, R. (1971) *The British Working Class and its Party: Preface* at http://www.workers.org.uk.

Carr, E.H. (1964) *What is History*, Harmondsworth, Penguin.

Davies, B. (1979) *In Whose Interests?: From Social Education to Social and Life Skills Training*, Leicester, NYB.

Ewen, J. (1972) *Towards a Youth Policy*, Leicester, MSB Publications.

James, S. (1975) *Race, Sex and Class*, New York, Falling Wall Press – available at http://libcom.org/library/sex-race-class-james-selma.

London-Edinburgh Weekend Return Group (1980) *In and Against the State*, London, Pluto.

Magri, L. (2008) 'The Tailor of Ulm', *New Left Review*, 51.

Nicholls, D. (2009) *Building Rapport: A Brief History of the CYWU*, London, UNITE/Bread Books.

Ratcliffe, R. (1987) *From CYSA to CYWU*, photocopied pamphlet distributed in 1987 within CYWU.

Workers, September 2009, *In Defence of the British Working Class* in Opinion at http://www.workers.org.uk/.

Primary Sources

Rapport: May, 1981; January, 1982; February, 1986; May, 1986; October, 1988; January, 1989.
Workers: September, 2009.

Radical youth work
Developing critical perspectives and professional judgement
By Brian Belton

'Whether you are a student, an academic, a youth worker, informal educator, community educator . . . I would strongly recommend this book.' *Youthlink Scotland.* 'What a breath of fresh air to read this book. It challenges the whole belief that someone can decide what is best for another person and then put in place what they think will bring the required change to make them into the 'citizens they should be', and questions the way in which youth work has become a tool of government conformity, rather than a means of journeying alongside young people as they grow . . . Not an easy or comfortable read as it pushes the brain to do some work, but definitely worth the effort.' *Youthwork*
978-1-905541-57-7

Journeying together
Growing youth work and youth workers in local communities
Edited by Alan Rogers and Mark K Smith

This accessible text explores a way of working, tested over 21 years in a UK-wide initiative, to grow youth work by supporting individuals to train professionally, while working in community-based organizations . . . and through this investment in people, to create lasting impact within communities. It is based on the 'Youth or Adult?' initiative, run by The Rank Foundation with YMCA George Williams College. It is founded on the belief that there is good in us all. This starting point makes change possible, and is backed up by the view that young people are members of communities – now, not at some point in the future, their voices must be heard, for the benefit of all and that there are leaders in the making amongst them.
978-1-905541-54-6

Essays in the history of youth and community work
Discovering the past
Edited by Ruth Gilchrist, Tony Jeffs, Jean Spence and Joyce Walker

'Dedicated to unravelling the many past aspects of youth and community work and providing an anchor for contemporary practice . . . The mix of contributions . . . range from narrative reflection to more conceptual and philosophical analysis . . . focus on both influential people and projects and movements . . . They engage with the wider politics and religion that influenced the development of youth and community work.' *Howard Williamson in Youth Work Now*
978-1-905541-45-4

Youth work process, product and practice
Creating an authentic curriculum in work with young people
By Jon Ord

Ord suggests that: 'Youth work cannot defend itself against erroneous and rival conceptions of practice unless it can sufficiently articulate its own. Through providing a framework for the creation of authentic curricula for youth work . . . this book offers one of the means by which individual workers, services and the profession as a whole can promote its unique educational practice.'
978-1-905541-11-9

Young people in post-conflict Northern Ireland
The past cannot be changed, but the future can be developed
Edited by Dirk Schubotz and Paula Devine

Covers not just what we expect to hear when NI is being discussed: violence, sectarianism, faith-segregated schooling, cross-community contact, politics, the peace process. But also: inward migration, mental health, suicide, bullying, pupil participation, sexual health, poverty, class, and how best to find out about these things in robust ways that involve young people in shaping the process.
978-1-905541-34-8

www.russellhouse.co.uk